SUPERNATURAL LORE OF SOUTHERN UTAH

SUPERNATURAL LORE OF SOUTHERN UTAH

DARREN M. EDWARDS

THE History PRESS

Published by The History Press
Charleston, SC
www.historypress.com

All photographs by the author unless otherwise noted.

First published 2022

Manufactured in the United States

ISBN 9781467150446

Library of Congress Control Number: 2022937944

Notice: The information in this book is true and complete to the best of our knowledge. It is offered without guarantee on the part of the author or The History Press. The author and The History Press disclaim all liability in connection with the use of this book.

For Diana Frances

"Adventure!"

CONTENTS

Acknowledgements 9
Introduction: Academic Approaches to the Supernatural 11

1. The Toquerville Challenge 15
2. The Ghosts of Southern Utah University 24
3. Where Rainbows Sleep: The Curse of Escalante Petrified Forest 44
4. The Haunting of the St. George Temple? 53
5. Route 666: The Devil's Highway 64
6. Keeping the Dead Alive: The Interesting Case of Lydia Knight 74
7. Grafton: Utah's Most Haunted Ghost Town 86
8. The Secrets of the Mountain Meadows Massacre 101
9. The Watson House 114
10. Skinwalkers and the Theft of Native American Beliefs 120
11. Odds and Ends 141

Notes 151
About the Author 160

ACKNOWLEDGEMENTS

First and foremost, I need to thank the people of Southern Utah. As I did the research for this book, the community responded time and again to my social media posts requesting stories or information. Please know that even if a story or detail you shared with me didn't make it into the book, it was still a crucial and helpful part of the research process. I especially want to thank all of the Native Americans who were willing to sit and share their stories and thoughts with me. Many of these stories and comments didn't make it into the final draft as direct quotes, but they are the scaffolding that holds up the stories that I did include.

While I wish I could thank the well over one hundred people I interviewed while researching the supernatural lore of Southern Utah, I owe a special thanks to Adrienne Gates, Ami Comeford, Aaron Timm, Thomas Braun, Shauri Lynne, Rick Atkin, Jayme Millett, Mika Fredrick, Cyndee Spilker-Jacobson, Kaye Feather Robinson, Mason Evan Runs Through, Philips Photography, Owen from Mexican Hat, Alexis Small, Marianne Hales Harding, Jessica T., Kristin Camille, Jennifer Brown Bennett, Autumn Rayanne, Ron and Barbara Harrison and Logan Graham for sharing their stories and thoughts with me.

I want to thank Dory Peacock of the *Ghost Box* podcast for her assistance with elements of research for the Southern Utah University and Kanab parts of the book. I also want to thank the librarians at the Gerald R. Sherratt Library at SUU for their help retrieving an image of the original article regarding Virginia Loomis.

I am especially indebted to Russ Beck, Jacoba Lynne Behunin, Ami Comeford, Angie Mace Merkley, Carly Olsen, Marianne Hales Harding, Christy Hall and Ron Coulson for their valuable feedback on early chapters of this book (and, of course, to Diana Frances, who heard everything in this book multiple times as I worked through drafts of each chapter).

Special thanks to my editors and everyone at The History Press.

As always, I must thank my family. Diana, thank you for your constant assistance, encouragement and understanding. If it weren't for your mental support, this book absolutely wouldn't have happened, and I'd probably be screaming in a corner somewhere. Mikey, thank you for letting me have a little extra time to myself when I needed to work on the book, and double thanks for all the snuggles and fun when I didn't. Again, Mom, Dad, thank you for helping me become who I am. And, of course, Ratatouille and Bear: you're good boys, *good boys*.

I owe a big thank-you to all of my students who sat through the various evolutions of my Academic Approaches to the Supernatural class over the years.

Lastly, thanks to all of the cultures represented in this book, especially the Native American cultures that have had to fight so hard against misrepresentation, appropriation and harmful legislation to survive.

INTRODUCTION

ACADEMIC APPROACHES TO THE SUPERNATURAL

My classroom is a second-floor corner room with windows that stretch nearly floor to ceiling. Sunrise to sunset, that room is awash with natural light. I've filled it with comfortable chairs (mostly armchairs, though there are a few rockers and one couch) because I want my students to feel comfortable. I like my classes—which include courses in research writing and in literature—to feel less like a study hall and more like a conversation at a friend's house or one of the French salons from the Enlightenment.

For the past four years, I've been teaching a full-year class titled Academic Approaches to the Supernatural. I don't know what students expect coming into the class, but there's a fair chance that it isn't what they're about to get.

The first half of the year in Academic Approaches to the Supernatural, we look at ghost stories, curses and urban legends from the perspective of a folklorist. That's actually where the idea for the class first germinated. During my graduate work at Utah State University, I had the great privilege of taking Folklore of the Supernatural from Dr. Jeannie Banks Thomas. In fact, I use a combination of the book she cowrote, *Haunting Experiences*, and Colin Dickey's *Ghostland* to guide students through that first semester. The first thing I tell my students is that we aren't interested in whether stories of hauntings, bigfoot, aliens, skinwalkers or zombies are factually true. What we *are* interested in is the cultural and personal truths such stories can help us explore. As Dickey notes in *Ghostland*, "More than just simple urban legends and campfire tales, ghost stories reveal the contours of our anxieties, the nature of our collective fears and desires, the things we can't talk about in any other way."[1]

I'm passionate about the approach to this first semester because supernatural lore is so often discounted. It is disregarded as trivial and as not worth serious, reflective, academic thought. As Diane E. Goldstein says, "The conventional academic point of view [is] that supernatural beliefs are survivals from a naive past and must decline as scientific thought ascends."[2] Often, when supernatural lore is given legitimate exploration, the only theme (inner story or deeper meaning) that people come up with is the now-worn-out "humans are afraid of the unknown," but these stories can teach us so much more about ourselves if we're willing to look at them with both an analytic eye and an open mind.

Throughout the first semester, we cover ideas stretching from gender issues in the burning of Bridget Cleary to the commodification of belief and the rise of digital urban legends. We explore the connections between supernatural lore and cultural representation, as well as the difference between that and cultural appreciation or appropriation. We discuss what these stories can tell us about both our collective guilt and our shared grief.

Much like the first semester, for the second half of the year, we don't concern ourselves with whether or not these stories are factually true; rather, we examine the methodology used by those who purport to investigate them. We start by discussing the scientific method and the difference between data and evidence. We look at the history of spirit photography, the story behind the discovery of the "fear frequency," the mythology of the Delphic Oracle and Pluto's Gate. I teach them about logical fallacies, confirmation bias and tricks like cold readings. I share stories from the history of spiritualism and séances.

We talk about Daniel Dunglas Home (pronounced *Hume*), a Scottish medium from the 1880s. Home awed crowds with feats from levitation to communing with the dead. In one particularly spectacular example, Home is said to have levitated out of one window and back in through another in broad daylight. That is what fascinates me about Home. Unlike the rest of the people involved in the spiritualist eruption of the 1800s, Home would perform in the light of day outside the walls of the darkened parlor. Darkness is a tool of the con artist and charlatan. It obscures and obfuscates. It replaces detail and data with atmosphere and lofty mystery.

Amongst this darkness, YouTube is littered with ghost hunters, "crypto" biologists and alien "researchers" who all try to fill their videos with the air of something academic. They create the illusion of scientific methodology. However, the substance and rigor of academia and the scientific community is nearly always missing. One of my favorite satirical ghost-hunting videos[3] points out that in every other scientific endeavor, you want to be able to see as much as possible, yet ghost-hunting sessions always take place at night, in the dark, where you can see less. That's why I'm so passionate about the ideas we explore in the second half of the year. The questions posed by supernatural lore and memorate (personal interactions with the supernatural) are among the most important questions humanity faces. What is the shape and breadth of reality? Is there something after this life? How do we cope with generational guilt or trauma? These are questions worth exploring properly. If we hope to learn the answers to these and so many other questions, we must be willing to look at them in the light. If we simply accept the answers produced with shoddy methodology because they're easy or they conform to what we want to believe, we're short-sheeting the lore, cheating our personal experiences and ignoring all of the questions those things can pose. Likewise, if we reject the stories as trivial, if we scoff rather than explore, we deny a central part of who we are.

If we are to make an honest assessment of this lore and these experiences, we must root ourselves in skepticism. Among those individuals and groups who believe in hauntings and monsters, skepticism gets a bad name. But it's a name unfairly earned. *Skeptic* is not a synonym for *disbeliever*. After all, disbelief is itself a form of belief. If belief in something's existence is one side of the supernatural coin, then disbelief is the other. A skeptic should stand firmly in the middle, surrounded by questions, unconvinced until one side or the other provides enough verifiable, reproducible, peer-reviewed evidence to sway them. As writer and professor emeritus of physics Chet Raymo says in his book *Skeptics and True Believers*, "Skeptics are children of the Scientific Revolution and the Enlightenment. They are always a little lost in the vastness of the cosmos, but they trust in the ability of the human mind to make sense of the world. They accept the evolving nature of truth and are willing to live with a measure of uncertainty....They are more interested in refining their own views than in proselytizing others."[4] Skeptics want to know what the data says. They want to know *if* things are true, not *that* they are true.

While I am firmly a skeptic, I am also a humanist. As such, I haven't written this book for the skeptic or for the true believer. I haven't written this book to pander or convert. By examining supernatural lore and memorate from a neutral stance, neither believing nor disbelieving, I hope to be more balanced in my approach to the questions they pose. I hope to create a work that, if nothing else, is honest in its approach to both gathering and exploring these stories.

SOME FINAL NOTES

While definitions of which areas are included in Southern Utah can vary wildly (for example, some categorizations include areas as far north as Moab), for the purposes of this book, I have defined Southern Utah as going from Iron, Garfield and San Juan Counties down to the southern border shared with Arizona.

There are some terms that it would be helpful for you to understand before starting the book.

FOLKLORE: a notion, story or saying that is widely circulated and preserved among a people.

LEGEND TRIPPING: "a name bestowed by folklorists and anthropologists on an adolescent practice (containing elements of a rite of passage) in which a usually furtive nocturnal pilgrimage is made to a site which is alleged to have been the scene of some tragic, horrific and possibly supernatural event or haunting."[5]

LIMINAL SPACES: a space that is neither here nor there—an in-between space. Bridges and tunnels are prime examples of liminal spaces; however, the idea can also extend to places that lie in between two stations of life. Cemeteries (a place for both the living and the dead) and schools (both the entrance and exit of the institution mark life transitions for students; thus, schools themselves are liminal) are examples of this.

MEMORATE: A personal narrative relating a notable experience, particularly one involving the supernatural.

There are some terms that I use interchangeably. Throughout the book, I use the terms *lore*, *narrative* and *story* primarily interchangeably; however, lore more often refers to something shared by more than one person, as in "local lore" versus a "personal narrative" or story. I also use the terms *urban legend* and *lore* or *folklore* interchangeably at times.

Likewise, I use the terms *Natives* (or *Native Americans*) and *Indigenous people* interchangeably. While also present in the book, the term *Indian* or *Indians* is almost always used in a historical context (I fully acknowledge that this is an outdated term that many Native individuals and communities find offensive).

Mormon, *Latter-day Saint* and *LDS* are also used interchangeably.

CHAPTER 1

THE TOQUERVILLE CHALLENGE

Take a walk down main street in Toquerville, Utah, on any fair-weather day, and you'll feel like you've been bumped into a painting of old small-town America. In fact, many of the homes in Toquerville are pioneer homes from the late 1800s and early 1900s. While there was a period of time when several of these historic homes had fallen into slight ill repair, most of them have been restored and beautified. They shine with lively colored trim (bright blues and whites aplenty), and they have lush flower gardens and well-trimmed lawns. Toquerville is white-picket Americana at its best. Even if—and maybe because—some of these homes have ghosts poking around inside of them.

The town itself was settled in 1858 when eight families were sent from Iron County by order of Mormon prophet and second president of the Latter-day Saint church, Brigham Young.[6] They moved in alongside the Paiute or Toquit Indians next to what is now called Ash Creek. According to the City of Toquerville website, the settlers named their town Toquerville after Chief Toquer, whom they considered "an enlightened Indian, friendly and with clean habits."[7] Surrounded by a mountain of black lava rock, the new settlement spread in a wide valley just off the creek. The city website also notes that in a 1868 article in the *Deseret News*, Toquerville is compared to "an oasis in an Arabian desert."[8]

While the town became known for its delicious figs, which you could buy a "hat full"[9] of for fifty cents, it never expanded like Cedar City to the north or St. George to the south. Nor did it dwindle and die off like the ghost towns of Silver Reef or Grafton. As Wes Larsen put it in *Historic Buildings Along Toquer Boulevard,* "Inasmuch as the adjacent land does not lend itself to agriculture, the town has grown very little and has retained the simple, quiet, and tranquil atmosphere of the early pioneer community." As a teenager, during family vacations to sunny St. George, I often heard my father joke about wanting to move to a little, middle-of-nowhere town, citing Toquerville as the example. Over one hundred years after it was settled by pioneers, the town had indeed changed very little.

In the summer of 1986, Aaron Timm was living with her family in a small, two-story home on main street in Toquerville. Aaron wasn't your typical southern Utah six-year-old. In a predominantly white, LDS area with a strong emphasis on conservative family values, Aaron would have stood out simply for not being a member of the LDS church, or for coming from a divorced household, or for having a Hispanic mother. But, on top of those things, Aaron was also legally blind and living with albinism. In the small town, she felt very much alone. As Aaron put it, "I was a buffet of everything shitty that you could be in Southern Utah." Standing out isn't always a bad thing, depending on why and how people react to you standing out. For Aaron, the ways she naturally stood out seemed to cause nothing but pain and loneliness. "The bullying," Aaron told me. "It was extremely terrible, and not just the kids, either, but the adults....I have very, very few positive memories of Southern Utah, precious few." Most of the children Aaron's age simply weren't allowed to be friends with her—a not-uncommon experience for non-LDS kids in an LDS community.

Then one night, as Aaron and her sister sat up talking, they looked across the street at the upstairs window of the Thomas and Mary Forsyth home, a stone pioneer home that had recently been vacated. For the first time in her life, Aaron saw something clear as day. As she said when I spoke with her, "One thing you need to understand about me is that I'm blind. So, the details that I saw of her, I shouldn't physically have been able to see from across the street with her being [in] the second-floor window. I shouldn't have seen what I saw. But I saw it." As to why she thinks she was able to see it, Aaron said, "I don't know, maybe I'm just cracked, but I think [I was able to see her] because she wanted to be seen. And so she's like, 'All right, I'm just gonna manifest in such a way that [she] can [see me].'" Aaron and her sister sat there in silence, both of them with eyes locked on the woman in white across the street. It wasn't a short vision, either. As Aaron recalls, the woman showed herself to the two girls for five minutes.

The woman's image is the only thing she's ever seen clearly, and Aaron recalls it in great detail. She remembers that the woman wore an old white lace nightgown that covered her from ankles to wrists. She was sitting in

Thomas Forsyth home from the side Aaron Timm would have first seen the woman in white.

front of a tall white candle and had long black wavy hair and blue eyes. For someone who once joked "Hell, I have to be pretty close to my husband to even recognize that it's him," spotting eye color from across the street is pretty impressive.

The fact that the woman appeared in the upstairs window is not uncommon. Along with liminal spaces, we tend to experience numinous things at the extremes of a space, like the attic or the basement. As folklorist Sylvia Ann Grider notes, "The attic and the basement are the extreme or most remote locations within the house and, therefore, the farthest from reality."[10] This is one of the reasons that so many of us sprint up the stairs after turning out the lights in the basement.

Thomas and Mary Forsyth built the home in 1865 when they moved from Santa Clara, Utah, thirty-three miles north to Toquerville. Thomas was born in Kelso, Roxburghshire, Scotland in 1813. After coming to the States, he joined the Mormon church in Nauvoo, Illinois, eventually making the trek west with the Steven Markham Company.[11] Upon arriving in the Salt Lake Valley, Thomas met and married his second wife, Mary Browett Holmes—his first wife, Isabella Donald, having passed away the year before. Once they moved to Toquerville, Thomas quickly established a shingle and sawmill. He also made wine, which he stocked in the home's basement until the LDS church forbade the drinking of alcohol. As Mary Phoenix notes in *Historical Buildings of Washington County*:

> *Forsythe was one of the finest vintners in the area, and he was particularly proud that his wine was used for sacramental purposes. Around the turn of the century, when the church ceased using wine in the services, it advised followers to get rid of all they had and produce no more. Forsythe didn't quite know what to do as the wine in his cellar was the finest he had ever produced, and it represented a great deal of money. But Forsythe did not need to worry. As soon as his wife, Mary, heard the edict read from the pulpit, she went home, slipped down beside the wine cache, and cut the pipes. When Forsythe went to inspect it, it had all drained away.*[12]

Eventually, the cute stone house was listed in the National Register of Historic Places, and as Wes Larsen points out, the house is "an excellent example of a 1½ story stone hall and parlor house whose projecting gable on the facade reflects Gothic Revival influences."

Aaron's miraculous vision of the woman in white in the upper window of the Forsyth home wasn't a singular event. Over the next couple of years, Aaron and her sister saw the woman in white half a dozen more times. Sometimes they saw her in the same upstairs window they first saw her in, sometimes in a downstairs window, and sometimes she appeared in the backyard, but always in summer. "Part of that might be that we stayed up later in the summer, for obvious reasons. And were outside with our parents and whatnot." Here is the thing, though; the ghost didn't scare them. For Aaron, it felt like the ghost was reaching out to her. The woman in white had chosen to reveal herself to Aaron because Aaron was special. As an outsider, that was something Aaron very much needed to feel. "We felt special. We're like, okay, we're badass, obviously, because she wanted us to see her." Telling the story to other kids bought Aaron a short burst of positive attention and a much-needed cessation, if only a temporary one, from bullying. Being invited to witness or take part in something supernatural makes us feel—forgive me—super. It makes us feel above what's natural or normal. It's as if the universe has singled us out, as if it saw something in us that the rest of the world missed.

This is one of the threads I've found running through so many memorate: we want these experiences to be special, extraordinary, miraculous. Occam's razor says that all things being equal, the simplest explanation is usually the right one, and most of us are glad to accept that scientific principle into our lives, except when it comes to those moments when we touch the supernatural. There is something inside us as human beings that longs to be part of something miraculous. And it is that desire for the miraculous that causes us to push away from Occam's razor when it comes to these experiences. If it was just a normal wind that made our normal door creak in our normal house, then we are simply normal, just like everyone else. But if it was a ghost reaching out from beyond visible reality to move a door in our haunted house, then we are part of something bigger than tangible, normal reality. We are apart from the boring masses trapped in the mundane experience of a simple world filled with concrete explanations. Still, research shows that, by and large, people are hesitant to share their supernatural experiences. A considerable part of that hesitance comes from a fear of standing out, of being seen as not normal.

I've been collecting both personal experiences with and broader folklore of the supernatural for at least the past six years, and I've found, time and again, that one of the elements at the center of these experiences is this longing for the miraculous. It could also be one of the reasons why we don't really want legitimate scientific inquiry into areas like ghosts and supernatural events, instead leaning on pseudo-science and confirmation bias. For too many of us, it seems, being able to prove or explain the supernatural would rob it of its mystery, would make it less miraculous, more ordinary. So, what do we do with these twin desires? In one of the most beautiful books I've ever read, *Still Life with Oysters and Lemon*, Mark Doty reflects on this idea while writing about the passion with which Dutch painters focused on the details of—of all things—lemons.

> *That lovely, perishable, ordinary thing, held to scrutiny's light, fixed in a moment of fierce attention. As if here our desire to be unique, unmistakable, and our desire to be of a piece were reconciled. Isn't that it, to be yourself and somehow, to belong? For a moment, held in balance.*[13]

Doty's prose suggests something of accepting ourselves wholly, seeing both the broad strokes that unite us all and the nuanced details that separate us as equally beautiful. Then again, there is another complicated intersection between being ordinary and standing out. Bullies targeted Aaron specifically because she stood out, but it was her outstanding experience with the lady in white that brought her a temporary moment of acceptance. Are there different shades of standing out, then, of being remarkable? Some studies suggest that up to 80 percent of people experience post-bereavement communications,[14] interactions of some kind with a recently deceased loved one, but few people talk about them because we fear how others will react (I explore these communications more in the chapter on Lydia Knight). The same experience that bought Aaron teenage street cred could function as a ding on the social credit and credibility of an adult. We want the spotlight but not the searchlight. We long for center stage, our five minutes of fame, to have our name lit up in lights, but we fear the looming crowd, the ticking clock and the pressure of all those lights. We want to be in others' thoughts, but we fear what those thoughts might be.

While it took over two decades, Aaron did eventually learn that she and her sister weren't alone in their experience with the woman in white. In a Facebook conversation I had with Aaron about the event, another gentleman from Toquerville responded that he, too, had seen a woman in white, and he even cited the same house without Aaron or I having mentioned it. Aaron stands out, then, but is not alone.

There is a cycle between urban legends, legend tripping and memorate that I discuss with my students (though I believe I may have first heard it from Dr. Jeannie Banks Thomas). We hear a story about someone, often an unnamed third person, who had something spooky happen to them at an old rundown house, or on a bridge, or in a tunnel. Our desire to experience something miraculous lights up, and we decide to visit the place for ourselves. When we get there, already in a mindset of wanting to experience something out of the ordinary, we have our own numinous experience. Whether the experience is really supernatural or not is of little consequence to the cycle, as we excitedly share the story with others in the appropriate setting—sitting around a campfire or chatting late at night in any eerie setting. The cycle repeats itself when people share our story and others decide to check it out for themselves. Stories that catch on like this tend to be the more widely told and thus more well-preserved lore. Perhaps this hints at another bridge between our desire to stand out and our desire to fit in. When we share our stories of the miraculous, do we share them in hopes that others will then join us? Do we want to stand together as we stand out against a normal life, a mundane existence?

One way that this cycle is prompted is through coming-of-age challenges. There is the typical "Do you dare to ring the doorbell on the haunted house?" trope we see so commonly in popular media (this is the premise for any number of movies and books, ranging from the *Goosebumps* stories to the 2016 film *Don't Knock Twice*). These challenges do more than provide an opportunity for us to show that we don't fear the darkness of the unknown; they give us

The home associated with the "bishop's house" or "murder house" lore.

a chance to discover for ourselves—at an age of self-discovery—where we stand in relation to that darkness.

Toquerville's coming-of-age challenge takes place little more than a block or two away from the home where Aaron Timm grew up. The story, sometimes called the "murder house" or the "bishop's house," revolves around a man who murders his wife and children in a gruesome and bloody manner, usually via stabbing. The challenge, often issued at a school bus stop near the house, is for kids to walk down the driveway of the house and get as close to the detached garage as they can. Aaron herself participated in the challenge:

> *It was kind of like a dare….You had to walk down this steep driveway that led to a detached garage, because something would happen to you there if you did…and I finally did it one day. The house was supposed to be haunted. The story that I heard was that a Mormon bishop had murdered his family in the house….There were two dares: you had to go look in the window, and you had to walk down this steep driveway that went to a detached garage. Because the story was that the driveway would fill with blood…and if you walked down far enough, you would see it fill with blood. So, we did it, and I saw it. Then when I looked in the window, I*

> *saw…all this old timey stuff. And to this day I don't know if that's what was really in the house or if it's what the house wanted to show me, because you talk to different kids and they all saw different things…So, like, I saw an old timey kitchen, you know…and other kids saw other things. But that was the dare you had to do. You were considered really cool if you went all the way down to the bottom of the driveway, which I did. So, I was kind of a badass for like a week.*

Aaron remembers seeing the driveway pool with blood, but she doesn't recall it with the same veracity as she does the woman in white. Reflecting on the two experiences, she said, "I'm not sure I quite believe the bishop's house stuff. Like, I might have just got caught up in it…but the woman in the stone house, I know she was real." As with Aaron's experience, these coming-of-age challenges offer a chance to stand out with some assurance that the attention garnered will be positive. Unlike an unprovoked encounter with the supernatural, where the story is so often ours alone, supernatural experiences spurred by a challenge become the community's story. We stand out while bringing others along for the ride.

In an attempt to see if these stories still lived on in the community that developed them, my son and I stopped in Toquerville to get pictures of the houses associated with them and talk to the locals about them. While the people now living across from the Thomas and Mary Forsythe home hadn't witnessed anything supernatural, my visit to the town hall found two receptionists and a FedEx delivery woman who recalled the "murder house." This falls in line with the established reasoning. Lore tied to a community, through something like a coming-of-age challenge, spreads farther and lives longer than individual memorate.

While I couldn't find any information on the building associated with the murder house (bishop's house), the lore behind it is culturally significant. One of the cornerstones of an LDS community is a belief in the patriarchal order and trust in the patriarch at the head of each institution, be it the church, the city or the home. In the story of the murder house, and even more directly when it's called the bishop's house, we find the representation of a cultural fear about what can happen when that patriarchal system breaks down and that trust is taken advantage of. The family should have been able to count on their father not only to protect them from outside dangers but also to lead them in making correct choices. Instead, the patriarch of the home abused his position and harmed—in this case, murdered—those under his stewardship. In a culture where so much trust is placed on the men in charge, there is always the potential for abuse, and it is natural for those told to follow to have anxiety about where they are being led. Thomas Forsyth felt this, if only for a moment, when church leaders told him to get rid of his wine. It would seem that Mary Forsyth also felt this anxiety when she rushed home to drain the wine in the cellar, perhaps unsure that the patriarch of her family, Thomas, would lead her where she felt she should be in regard to the church's declaration.

Whether we stand out alone or together, we should stand sure in our own worth. It shouldn't take something defying our understanding of reality to reinforce our understanding of our own value. At times we may find ourselves supported by the arms of a community, and at times, as with Aaron, we may stand outside of those arms. When we find ourselves ousted by a community, as almost all of us will at one time or another, we should examine the differences that separate us from others. If we do that, if we hold "that lovely, perishable, ordinary thing, held to scrutiny's light, fixed in a moment of fierce attention" as Mark Doty suggests, we will find that the miraculous is closer than we thought.

CHAPTER 2

THE GHOSTS OF SOUTHERN UTAH UNIVERSITY

Universities are the perfect place for ghosts, if you think about it. They are, by their very nature, liminal spaces. They are not a place where people are meant to stay. Every four years, another cadre of eager young students makes its way onto campus, providing a fresh opportunity for faculty, staff and other locals to share their unique lore with a virgin audience. And when it comes to ghost stories, Southern Utah University (SUU) in Cedar City, Utah, sits at the head of the class. From ghosts driven to avenge their murder to those who were robbed of their chance to perform on stage in life to a librarian who can't seem to give up the school and the students he grew to love, the SUU campus is virtually bubbling with ghosts.

Dr. John Laurence Seymour

At around six years old, I sat down to watch the original *Ghostbusters* movie, totally unprepared for what I was about to experience. In the opening scene, a flock of birds scatters as the camera slowly pans down to a statue of a lion sitting outside the main branch of the New York Public Library. Inside, we find an archetypal librarian pushing a cart of books through a room filled with patrons reading at long, wooden tables. As the scene shifts, we find our librarian slowly walking down a narrow and poorly lit staircase and into a darkened room filled with row after row of bookshelves. Eerie music

The front of SUU's Old Main building as it stands today.

starts to rise in volume as she runs her fingers along the stacks. Near the end of the aisle, unbeknownst to our dear librarian, books begin to float from shelf to shelf behind her head. As she turns down another aisle, card catalogs begin to slide open as she passes them, cards shooting out of them as they do. Alerted by the sound of cards flying through air, she turns to see a ticker-tape parade of bibliographies. Startled, she turns and begins running back through the rows, which feel as if they've become a maze. As she turns another corner, the camera closes in on her face, which has suddenly drawn tight in fear. She freezes in place.

Six-year-old me couldn't look away from the screen, but it wasn't until our heroes, the Ghostbusters, explored the library that I got to see what had terrified the librarian. In one second (I timed it), the purple, glowing ghost of a woman grew and turned into an almost ape-like skeletal figure rushing toward the camera. The next thing I knew, our heroes were sprinting down the front steps of the library, and I was curled up in the fetal position. The scene gave me nightmares for weeks, and even later in life, walking through the stacks of Utah State University's Merrill Library late at night, I would feel chills and discomfort thinking about the scene. Unlike *Ghostbusters'* iconic library ghost, the spirit who haunts the Gerald R. Sherratt Library on the SUU campus isn't very, well, haunty.

Before it was the Electronic Learning Center, this building housed the SUU library and the ghost of Dr. John Laurence Seymour.

The new Gerald R. Sherratt Library, where Dr. Seymour's ghost moved along with the books in 1995.

Dr. John Laurence Seymour, who served as the head librarian from 1969 to 1985,[15] is said to hang around the library as a positive force, kept there simply by his love for his books, the school and its students. In fact, according to an article on the SUU website, the doctor "resides in his very own office in the special collections section of the library."[16] The article goes on to say that he was a "famous American composer and playwright," which is a simplified if not distortedly rosy version of things.

Early in his career, Seymour both taught at Berkeley and served as the head of the drama department at Sacramento Junior College.[17] In 1935, his most notable work, a one-act play called *Pasha's Garden* that had been awarded the Bispham Memorial Medal Award, premiered at the Metropolitan Opera. Seymour was, and is to this day, the only member of the Church of Jesus Christ of Latter-day Saints to have a show performed at the Met.[18] However, the opera received poor reviews and ran for only three performances; one critic called the show "just plain silly"[19] and another "a monumental disaster."[20] A *TIME* magazine review of the play from just after it premiered stated that Dr. Seymour's play "established an all-time record for dullness and ineptitude."[21] It would seem Dr. Seymour took the criticism understandably hard. It would be years before he composed again. Instead, in 1940, he earned his PhD in English literature from Berkley. And in 1969, Dr. Seymour moved to Cedar City to take up a position as a librarian at SUU.

By all accounts, Dr. Seymour cherished his time at SUU. Maybe it was finally being in a community that was composed primarily of people of the same faith. Maybe it was going from being a small fish in a big bowl to a big fish in a small bowl, or maybe it was something else—maybe he'd just found a community that accepted and loved him openly. Whatever the reason, it would seem that Dr. Seymour loved his position so much that he decided to stay with the students and books of SUU forever.

Little Miss

Unlike Dr. Seymour, not all of SUU's ghosts are friendly. In fact, this list grows considerably grimmer as we move through it. Where Dr. Seymour stayed connected to the school because of his love for it, others, like Little Miss, seem stuck on campus due to the tragic nature of their death. The story of Little Miss takes place much earlier in the school's history. Sometime around the early 1900s, a young girl (stories vary as to her age, anywhere from eight to sixteen) was using a piano on the third floor of Old Main to practice for a performance.[22] However, at least one version has the whole story taking place in Braithwaite Fine Arts Gallery back when it served as an auditorium.[23] Another difference is that some of these accounts say she was practicing for a piano recital, others that she was preparing to give a performance at her prom.[24] In either version, Little Miss never got to give her performance. Whether by stroke, heart attack or ruptured appendix, she died right there on that piano bench midway through Joe Loss's "Deep Purple." There are several reports of people hearing the tune playing on the third floor of Old Main (and also in the Braithwaite) late at night. Mary Jane Smith shared her experience on Facebook:

> *Old Main IS haunted. When I was taking a night class at SUU in 2002, a group of us were studying in Old Main when we heard someone playing music, sounded like a piano, VERY loudly on the floor above us—there was no one in the building! We gathered our things as quickly as possible & got out of there! Definitely someone was in that building that night trying to scare us, and it worked.*

Other stories hold that it's bad luck to play "Deep Purple" at prom—though I don't know that's been much of a risk since the 1950s.

The Ballerina and the Top Hat Man

Little Miss isn't the only ghostly performer who was denied their chance to perform (which makes sense for a school with a heavy focus on theater—SUU is home to the Utah Shakespeare Festival). In fact, she isn't even the only ghost with a connection to the song "Deep Purple." According to an article in *Iron County Today*, the haunting song actually accompanied a ballerina—not a pianist—who never had a chance to perform because she died from an infected blister on her toe after practicing too long into the night.[25] At least, that's one version of the story. I talked to a number of SUU students who told me a different version.

According to them, if you happen to be walking past the Adams Memorial Theater (located very close to Old Main) late at night, you just might hear the delicate tapping of feet from SUUs Phantom Ballerina. In yet another

The Adams Memorial Theater is home to several ghosts.

version, this one found in the university's promotional *Bird Book*, a jealous husband murdered the ballerina when he found her dancing with another man in the tunnels that run between the theater and the auditorium:

> *Long ago, a jealous husband of a ballerina walked through the tunnels. When he looked through a grate, he had a perfect view of the stage and saw his wife dancing with another man. In a fit of rage, he murdered his wife and the unknown man. Soon after, he committed suicide due to his overwhelming grief. Today, if you walk down the tunnels, you can sometimes see a lovely ballerina dancing on the moonlit stage.*[26]

This iteration of the story notes the husband's motivation was jealous rage; however, in the versions where the boyfriend murders the dancer, the storytellers never mention a reason for the murder.

Domestic violence is a common motive cited when exploring the backstory of hauntings. That stories based on domestic violence fill our urban legends and local lore speaks to a dark truth we aren't comfortable talking about in more direct ways. But these uncomfortable truths are so often the most important for us to discuss openly. Back in 2016, I wrote an essay about this idea. In discussing sex crimes and domestic violence, I noted that "in so many ways, our silence…is getting people killed."[27] This collective squeamishness about discussing things like domestic violence only enables its perpetrators. As folklorist Jeannie Banks Thomas notes:

> *These ghostly depictions mirror a too-common social pattern of male violence and domestic violence. Some research indicates that women also use violence in intimate relationships, but at nowhere near the same rates or severity. Statistics from the U.S. Department of Justice reveal that women undergo more than ten times as many incidents of violence by intimates than do men.*[28]

Almost more telling than the difference in the amount of violence between men and women is the difference in the reasons for violence. Banks Thomas goes on to highlight this point, using research from professor of sociology Kersti Yllö that "found that men are more likely to use domestic violence instrumentally: for terrorizing women to obtain compliance and passive acceptance." In contrast, women tend to use violence primarily in self-defense or to express anger, not to control or manipulate.

A locked gate of the Adams Memorial Theater.

Is this the chalky handprint of a student, or could it be the ghostly prints of the top hat man inside the Adams Memorial Theater?

Looking up at the back row of the Adams Memorial Theater from the stage.

In a unique and interesting twist to the usual "boyfriend murders girlfriend" trauma-trapped ghost story, the Phantom Ballerina's story adds a third and mysterious figure. A shadowy man in a black top hat, who is not assumed to be the boyfriend or husband, watches the ballerina as she makes her ethereal pliés and pirouettes. While not the romantic partner, this figure, who can be seen near the back row late at night, is protective and jealous of the dancer. Several versions of the story say that the man will become angry if anyone else tries to watch the ballerina's performance.

While he is often seen in association with the ballerina, the top hat man has been cited on his own in places other than the Adams Memorial Theater or the tunnels below. MacKenzie Skye Pedersen experienced such an encounter late one night in the auditorium theater where she was helping with the production of *A Funny Thing Happened on the Way to the Forum*. She shared her story on Dory Peacock's podcast *The Ghost Box*:

> *Now the set for this show…was, I believe, two doors on the bottom, but I vividly remember there were four doors across the top….Lots and lots of doors on this set. The person I was dating at this time had a key to get into the auditorium, and we thought it would be fun to go into the auditorium and just sneak in….I didn't think anything would actually happen. So, it's late at night. It's probably one-thirty, two in the morning on Halloween eve. He unlocks the door, and we sneak in. I kind of had a crush on this guy, so I was like, "Oh my gosh! This is so scary! Oh my gosh!" So, our whole goal was to walk up the right-hand aisle of the auditorium, cross in front of the stage, and then go back up the far left aisle, leaving the aisle in the middle untouched. We weren't going to go up that aisle.*
>
> *So, first thing we do is get in, and it just has a really dead feeling. Like it was too quiet. It just felt really weird. And it was all fun and games. And we were walking up the right-hand aisle, and we got this weird feeling that someone else was in here. And I looked at the stage, and you couldn't really see anything on the stage, except the ghost light* [a lone light left hanging on an unoccupied stage as a safety measure to stop workers from stumbling over props and sets] *was far away. It was in the wings, so there was this tiny, tiny dim light casting the whole set in this shadow, but we could see all the doors were open on the set.*
>
> *So, as we get to the front of the theater, we both stopped giggling because we both felt the same thing, and it just felt like someone was there. And we were like, "Oh shhh, let's just get this over with. Let's just get out of here." So, we were still walking our kind of slow pace, and we got to the very*

The auditorium theater where MacKenzie Skye Pedersen had her run-in with the top hat man.

middle of the stage, and suddenly all of the doors start slamming on the set. Even if someone was back there, there's no way they could have got to all of those doors. It was a double-decker set; there's no way they could have started slamming all of the doors.

At that point, we freaked out, I started screaming, and we bolted up the middle aisle. Because this dark presence was there, and it was like, "Get out." I didn't see anything at that point except the doors slamming. We bolted out. So, we get out of the auditorium, and then the box office is off to the right-hand side, and the doors to the outside are made of glass, you can totally see through them. So, me and this guy burst through the glass doors. And we're just running for our car. Our car was just down the grassy front part of the theater; it was facing the glass doors. We jump in the car and lock all the doors. And we look up, and there is a dark figure standing in the middle of the glass doors, staring at us. I couldn't see any facial features. It didn't have solid physical definition that I could see. It was just a dark humanoid figure, but we could clearly see that he had that hat on, that hat silhouette. We lost our damn minds and drove away.

McKenzie's story hits a couple of common notes. Many urban legends revolve around amorous teens and young adults going someplace late at night to spend time alone. Before they get much time together, however, a supernatural force interrupts the outing, sending the couple running. Stories that fit this pattern typically express cultural fears associated with chastity and unsupervised youth, the idea being that if you're somewhere you shouldn't be, doing something you shouldn't be doing, bad things will happen. However, when used as a warning story of sorts, these types of urban legends tend to be centered on an unnamed third person. "There were these two kids who went out to Make-out Point…" But, here, with McKenzie's story, we have a firsthand experience, setting it apart from typical "teens where they shouldn't be" trope.

According to a *Cedar City News* article, members of the Southern Utah Paranormal Society (SUPS) have also had multiple experiences in the auditorium and the tunnel that connects it to the Adams Memorial Theater. In one example, Charlisa McConnell-Robertson, an SUPS member, reported being pushed in the back by a ghost while walking through the tunnels during a live performance.[29]

THE SEAMSTRESS'S DAUGHTER

Not all the deaths that have kept spirits bound to SUU were the result of murder. One batch in particular was caused by neglect. Between the Adams Memorial Theater and the original SUU Auditorium runs a tunnel through which performers could move from one stage or dressing room to the other as needed. There roams the ghost of an unknown girl who was left after hours, forgotten in the lower levels by her parents. Some of the "neglected child" ghost stories come with more background and depth than the others. The most detailed story places the blame for neglect on the shoulders of a mother employed by the university as a costume maker. After bringing her little girl with her to campus, the seamstress, caught up in her work, let the girl wander away into the bowels of the theater and tunnels. Alone and curious, the girl inspected the machinery—I picture stage ropes and pulleys. She caught her coat in the riggings and was subsequently killed. At least one student told me that performers at the Adams Theater believe that the last person to leave the dressing room for the day must say goodbye to the little girl, or the dressing room will be a mess the next morning, and the show will be cursed. This superstition also makes an appearance in the university's 2016–17 press book:

Statue of William Shakespeare on SUU campus.

> *No one knows much about her or her past life, but what we do know is that she lives in the dye room and isn't one to mess with. Every night before leaving, you must say "Good night, little girl," and lock the dye room doors or else she will sabotage shows.*[30]

Theaters are superstitious places by nature. The Boston University Theater is haunted by its founder, Henry Jewett; the ghost of "the most beautiful girl in New York," Olive Thomas, still walks the halls of the New Amsterdam Theater, carrying the blue bottle of mercury pills she used to take her life. Turning off the ghost light before leaving the theater is considered bad luck. You should never give a performer flowers before a show, and, of course, you never wish a performer good luck. Simply tell them to break a leg. But theatrical superstition isn't the only thing we can take away from the story of the seamstress's daughter. We see here a little girl who is denied the protective attention of her mother and now demands it from the performers whom her mother seemed to place above her. We also see what Banks Thomas refers to as "the deviant femme."

From precolonial times through the "cult of true womanhood" in the 1960s, society has told us that a woman's traditional role is in the home with the family. Her duty is to protect the children. Often, in folklore featuring female ghosts, we see a deviation from this role and a destruction of the traditional concept: the old spinster who never married and lives in the big spooky house all by herself, thus shunning her social duty to marry and reproduce; the teenager who forsakes her purity for a trip to lovers' lane; the mother who murders her own children. These all show this deviation from the cultural norm. As Colin Dickey notes in *Ghostland*, "Ghosts, you could say, flock to women left alone."[31]

VIRGINIA LOOMIS

While the deviant femme may play against traditional feminine roles, its parallel pushes into the worst of male stereotypes and cultural characteristics. A whole category of supernatural lore can be lumped together under the simple label "toxic masculinity." Much like the Phantom Ballerina, many of these stories start with the jealous/controlling male figure (boyfriend or husband) who lashes out and murders his partner, leaving the traumatized female's ghost to seek justice or revenge.

SUU's Old Main from the spot where students stand to spot the ghost of Virginia Loomis.

A perfect example of this can be seen in SUUs most well-known ghost, Virginia Loomis. Walking around SUU campus on a crisp fall day, nearly everyone I stopped to talk to knew the story of Virginia Loomis. In fact, according to an article on Backpackerverse.com, students used to tell the story to freshmen during campus tours before the administration stepped in and stopped them.[32] To this day, students gather in front of Old Main each October to have a hot chocolate social and see if they can—as the lore holds—see Virginia in the third-floor window on a full moon at the stroke of midnight.

A ghostly apparition appearing in an upstairs window at the stroke of midnight would be enough to fuel lore for a long time, but an apparition with pyromaniacal tendencies—that's how you become a legend of epic proportions.

SUU (then the Branch Normal School) was founded in 1897, and the first building (Old Main) was built in 1898. The timber for the building had to be hauled down from the mountains through steep and treacherous snowdrifts, but it's with the stones used for the building that our story starts.

It was at the quarry that sandstone came from that Steven Farr is said to have violently killed Virginia Loomis. As we've seen in these narratives, many ghost stories are vague when it comes to the fine details. The Phantom Ballerina was murdered by her boyfriend, no mention of the specific method. But Farr didn't just murder Virginia. He slit her throat and left her with her back bent over a boulder, where she bled out over the stone. Later, those same stones would be used to build Old Main, thus attaching Virginia's ghost to the building.

Though he'd left town after getting away with Virginia's murder, years later, Farr returned and found employment as the furnace worker in the basement of Old Main. Quick to act, Virginia caught Farr's arm in the furnace door on his first night of work, burning him alive and Old Main to the ground. Despite exacting her revenge, Virginia still haunts the halls of the rebuilt Old Main building.

The earliest version of the story I could track down dated to 1986. This version of the story makes several interesting claims. It specifies that Virginia's throat was slit with a handsaw. It claims that the school brought in a professor of parapsychology from the University of Utah in Salt Lake City. Dr. Jerode Spear (of whom I could find no record, nor any record of the university having a parapsychology department) investigated the rubble of Old Main and found that Virginia had indeed exacted her revenge. Despite the lack of

Many of the stones from the original Old Main were incorporated into the new building and still bear the burn marks from the fire.

records for either Spear or a parapsychology department at the university (the first result in a Google search for "University of Utah Parapsychology Department" is a link to a version of the Virginia Loomis story), this aspect of the story continues in most modern iterations of the lore.

The '86 version of the legend reads more like a short story than a news article. In the '86 article, the author, Tom Braun, claims to have been given access to Spear's never-before-seen notes from the investigation:

> *Dr. Spear's findings have never been made public. His notes and diary with which he prepared his report of SUSC* [Southern Utah State College] *officials were obtained from his estate by his grandson, a student at SUSC.*

Quoting several dramatic segments from Spear's notes, Braun is able to add a level of detail to the story that makes it feel more theatrical than folkloric. In one passage, Braun quotes Spear describing his exploration of the burned ruins of Old Main:

> *As I climbed down into the gutted and blackened basement of Old Main, a chill ran up my back. I felt a cold and deadly presence. I turned my head slowly and looked about me fully expecting to see a ghost. But I didn't. I did, however, see an old coal furnace sitting in the center of a large room. The feeding door was shut but something was sticking out of its door jam. I wrenched it free and held in my hand a charred human bone.*[33]

There are a few notable and interesting points here. First and foremost, the idea that someone died during the 1948 fire of Old Main. In all the non-supernatural accounts of the fire that I could dig up, there was not one mention of anyone dying in the fire, let alone a furnace worker by the name of Stephen Farr. This is not to say that nothing was lost in the fire. As one article on the history of the fire notes, "Art professor Mary L Barstow's paintings, a lifetime of work, were completely destroyed in the fire. Only about 20 percent of the library collection had survived the fire."[34] The loss of the building itself, a building the entire town had banded together to build, carried a heavy grief.

Perhaps the most interesting part of Braun's '86 article is the very last paragraph. One simple line. Two words, barely visible on the grainy microfiche that everyone who has pulled from the article seems to have missed somehow. From students who stumbled upon it when looking for

THE THUNDERBIRD TUESDAY OCTOBER 28, 1986 PAGE 7

THE HAUNTING OF OLD MAIN

BY TOM BRAUN

You are dead. You were killed violently—your throat was ripped open with a handsaw—and now your body s in a grave decomposing.

You know who killed you, yet your killer is free.

You are a spirit and have been offered eternal rest in paradise, but you reject the offer. You will not have rest...but revenge.

Having spurned eternity for vengeance, you have entered a new dimension. You have entered the realm of spirits that live neither on earth nor in paradise. You are in a state of limbo. You are a ghost.

And every ghost must have its haunt.

You might consider haunting Old Main on the SUSC campus.

You will not be the first ghost nor the only ghost to haunt Old Main, according to Dr. Jerode Spear, professor of parapsychology at the University of Utah.

Dr. Spear was hired in 1948 by SUSC officials after poltergeist activity in Old Main terrified the community. The supernatural phenomena resulted in the execution death of one man and the fire gutting of Old Main.

Dr. Spear's findings have never been made public. His notes and diary from which he prepared his report for SUSC officials were obtained from his estate by his grandson, a student at SUSC.

What you are about to read are excerpts from those notes and the diary. They constitute the only comprehensive documentation of murder and destruction in America by supernatural beings from the "dark side."

From the notes of Dr. Spear:

I believe the haunting of Old Main began during its construction in 1898 and has continued unabated for over 50 years.

During the laying of the foundation, a laborer was guiding a large sandstone into place when the word "Virginia" appeared in human blood on the sandstone. (The stone with its inscription can be seen in the special collections section of the SUSC Library.)

Supernatural activity occurred so frequently after Old Main was completed that it was common knowledge among SUSC faculty and students that Old Main was haunted. Ghostly apparitions were seen nightly; unearthly lights glowed from third story windows; floating shadows swirled around the belfry; and most famous, a quiet melodious fluting began precisely at midnight and continued until 1 a.m.

Among my colleagues who study supernatural phenomena it is a documented fact that once a structure becomes the home of a spirit, that structure acts as a conduit between the phantom dimension and our world. It becomes a haunt for exiled spirits—A legion of devils.

I believe that is what Old Main has become—a door from the world-of-spirits to our world. A door that burst open recently with devastating results.

On December 12, 1948 at 7:30 a.m. a spirit from the phantom world thrust through the veil and killed to exact vengeance. And then, as if a finale, Old Main burned. I firmly believe that the hands that ignited the blaze were not of this world.

From the diary of Dr. Spear:

As I climbed down into the gutted and blackened basement of Old Main a chill ran up my back. I felt a cold and deadly presence. I turned my head slowly and looked about me fully expecting to see a ghost. But I didn't. I did however see an old coal furnace sitting in the center of a large room. The feeding door was shut but something was sticking out of its door jamb. I wrenched it free and held in my hand a charred human bone.

In front of the furnace lay a large bell like those found on top of some churches, and protruding from beneath it—a human skeleton. I rolled the bell aside exposing the remainder of the skeleton. My eyes were pulled to the blackened skinless skull. On its forehead I saw an inscription. It read 'VIRGINIA.' It appeared to be written in human blood by a finder.

Inside the furnace I found the remains of a human hand and wrist.

Finding nothing else I sat on the bell to meditate. As I pondered the evidence, I could feel supernatural forces. Emotions still hung heavy in the air. And then suddenly I felt what had happened here: The bones I found belong to a John Moore. On the morning of the fire Mr. Moore was shoveling coal into the furnace when something slammed the furnace door shut on his arm. He was pinned. His hand and forearm burst into flame inside the furnace. (When he screamed he heard laughing. When he fainted Old Main filled with cheers and applause. But who would cheer a dying man?) The fire spread from his arm to his sleeve, ignited his hair, and began melting his face. He was still fighting to free himself as he burned. Hanging from the furnace door and engulfed in flames he became the torch that spread the fire to the spilled coals on the basement floor. The fire moved upward finally reaching the roof and belfry. As the belfry burned and began to collapse something rang the bell for the last time. It then crashed through Old Main's three floors and landed on what was left of Mr. Moore.

Whatever killed Mr. Moore smeared the word 'VIRGINIA' on his skull, with his own blood.

From the notes of Dr. Spear:

There is a supernatural link with the burning and killing. In 1896—two years before Old Main was built—A beautiful 16-year-old lady, Virginia Loomis, was murdered east of Cedar City in the red hills. Her throat had been slashed and her blood soaked body lay draped over a large red sandstone boulder.

Her killer was never found though a young man, Steven Farr, went to trial for the slaying. He was acquitted for lack of evidence.

In 1898, the foundation stones for Old Main were out from the same red sandstone boulder Virginia was killed on.

I believe Virginia chose to remain in limbo to hunt her killer, and when the sandstone upon which she ws killed became the foundation of Old Main, she moved in and became Old Main's first permanent ghost.

When I was in the basement I scraped some blood from Mr. Moore's skull and sent it to a lab. The report confirmed a suspicion I had had. The blood on the skull was not Mr. Moore's. In fact—the skull was not Mr. Moore's. The man killed in Old Main was Steven Farr—the same Steven Farr who had been acquitted 50 years earlier for Virginia's murder.

My investigation revealed that Mr. Farr left Cedar City the day after his acquittal and had returned just two weeks before the fire. He had taken the part-time job tending the furnace of Old Main.

Virginia knew her killer, and when he entered her haunt for his first day of work on that fateful morning—she killed him.

According to Dr. Spear's notes, he included a warning at the end of his official report which he presented to SUSC officials on Dec. 22, 1948 as a "Christmas present."

"Though Old Main is gutted by fire, she retains an eerie unnatural presence. The fire did not destroy the conduit from the phantom world. I recommend Old Main be torn down. If you do not do it, you have been forewarned. Tragedy could strike again."

Is Old Main really haunted as Dr. Spear suggested some 38 years ago? Do the sightings persist? Can one hear the melodious fluting from midnight to 1 a.m.? And are there really footsteps that can be heard but not seen? Well, perhaps, because as you know, "every ghost must have its haunts."

(Just kidding.)

The original article "The Haunting of Old Main," written by Tom Braun in 1986. *Courtesy of SUU Special Collections.*

spooky stories to journalists writing up articles on local haunts just in time for Halloween, no one seems to have cited those weighty last words, "Just kidding."

And what do we do with that? And why do I bring it up at all? I said in my introduction that I have no interest in exploring the factual accuracy of supernatural lore, and I have no desire to be the party pooper who pisses on the biggest spectral fire in Cedar City, the lore that everyone knows, that draws people together for hot chocolate socials. Still, I hold firm to the belief that whenever the factual truth and the emotional or, let's say, cultural truth seem to be in conflict, one should certainly not ignore the facts, nor should they abandon the emotion; rather, they should explore the fertile ground that lies in between the two.

In that spirit, I found and reached out to Tom Braun, who, it turns out, still lives in Cedar City. I asked Tom if anybody had reached out to him since he wrote the original article thirty-eight years ago. "No. You're the first one," he told me. Before I could continue exploring the creation of the story, I had to get confirmation. Was Virginia real or just a figment of his imagination? "Yeah…Virginia was made up," he replied. The statement hung for a moment as I pondered the gravity of what he'd just said. Then he added, "I was front page editor for the college paper, and we needed a Halloween story." Where had the idea come from? "If I recall, some kids in one of the English classes said they saw lights up in Old Main, and I heard about some tunnels between the theaters that were supposed to be haunted." These vague notions of haunted spaces gave birth to a detailed story that became an urban legend with a life of its own. Tom went on to tell me about his kids and grandkids coming to him each year around Halloween to let him know that people were still telling his story.

Tom had seen some of the recreations of his story over the years, but I didn't think to ask him if he knew about the hot chocolate socials, or the kids going ghost hunting or the university using the story for marketing. I wish I had. He told me with a laugh that the Virginia story was the worst thing he'd ever written. Still, it may turn out to be the most important, because there was something in it that resonated with the community. As Dickey notes, for a ghost story to really gain traction, "there's often significant embellishments and fabrication before they catch on in our imagination, and teasing out these alterations is key to understanding how ghosts shape our relationship to the past."[35] I could speculate about the cultural truths the story may have spoken to that made it grow the way it did, but honestly, with this one, I think I'd rather focus on the back end of things, on what the story has done—the dorm-room friendships built over late-night ghost stories, the romances started when freshmen met up in front of Old Main on a full moon, the way the story of Virginia has woven itself into the fabric of the university and the school spirit of its students and alumni.

I told Tom how rare it is to track a piece of folklore back to its origins. It's a bit like finding the pot of gold at the end of the rainbow—or, I suppose, the beginning.

So, does knowing that the story isn't real ruin it? Should people stop looking for Virginia in the upstairs windows of Old Main? Does knowing the origin of a rainbow, the sunlight hitting raindrops, ruin the wide spread of colors that come from it? I hope that people keep talking about Virginia, sharing her story, thinking about the issues—like domestic violence—it raises. I hope generations still find themselves lost in the lore and the way it has grown and morphed over time, filling minds in Cedar City with color and wonder.

CHAPTER 3

WHERE RAINBOWS SLEEP

The Curse of Escalante Petrified Forest

As time has moved forward, humans have found ever more sophisticated ways of counting the passage of that time. From sundials and water clocks to quartz crystal clocks and the ever-evolving variety of atomic clocks, we have found more and more exacting measurement systems. We've also discovered a plethora of ways the earth itself seems to keep time: rings in trees, layers of rock, radiometric decay. It is easy to get lost in the exactness of this type of data. If we're not careful, we can lose the feeling of time among the data of time. As impressive and important as it is to know that the trees in the Escalante Petrified Forest are potentially 155 million years old, the number doesn't convey the way that amount of time feels when we are confronted with the physical representation of it.

Escalante Petrified Forest State Park opened to the public in 1976. One of the smaller state parks in Utah (1,350 acres)[36] when compared to the likes of Snow Canyon (7,400 acres) or Sand Hollow (20,611 acres), Escalante feels approachable, even cozy. That might also be why it's one of the more overlooked state parks. Surrounded by superstar parks like Zion National Park and Bryce Canyon National Park and just a short drive from Grand Canyon National Park and Monument Valley, it's easy to see how Escalante could slide by tourists' radar unnoticed. Still, this little park has a beauty and mystique worth stopping to experience. Perhaps more than any of the parks I've listed above, Escalante Petrified Forest State Park feels old. I mean, I get that all of the parks are really the same age, but time seems to have a different

Petrified wood at Escalante Petrified Forest State Park.

quality at Escalante, a different texture. Visitors digest time differently than they might at a larger, more crowded park. But it's not just the absence of other people that makes Escalante move a bit more like the damp sand left after a flash flood. The petrified wood for which the forest is named has an almost magnetic force, as if in those blocks of what were once wood, one can feel time slowed enough to become tangible.

If I try to picture a mad scientist concocting a plot to freeze time, I imagine it would look somewhat like the process nature actually goes through to create petrified wood. Twisting a handlebar mustache, the scientist would croak, "Flood it all and rip the trees out. Bury them in mud!" Petting his hairless cat, he'd go on to explain how he would inject water into the buried trees, but since they'd be encased in a vacuum, the wood wouldn't rot. Instead, the silica in the groundwater would slowly replace the trees' natural organic material, thus transforming the tree into something new, yet leaving the shape of the tree unchanged, like some arboreal version of *Invasion of the Body Snatchers*.

Or, slightly less dramatically, as the park brochure puts it:

> *Groundwater permeated the buried trees over millions of years. Because they were in an oxygen-free environment, the trees did not decay. Instead, through a complex geologic process, silica solution in the groundwater replaced organic material in the tree, leaving the cell structure intact. Due to erosion, this fallen forest of petrified trees is now exposed.*[37]

The "complex geologic process" leaves the now-petrified wood glowing in vivid bands of color. The hills of Escalante are covered in petrified wood, from small, pocket-sized pieces to entire trees—though it is the pocket-sized ones that people find tempting. I get it. In addition to their beauty, there is something mystical about these tiny frozen pieces of time. With such light traffic, there is no one to notice if you stoop to snag a little souvenir. Or is there?

I visited Escalante Petrified Forest State Park on an overcast day, a day after there had already been some flooding. Hiking paths and flood runoff paths looked confusingly similar. Before I even reached the noticeable bulk of the petrified wood, I already felt as if I was standing in a temporally diffused zone. Maybe it was something about the juniper trees, the way the bark curls off in large papyrus-like flakes, the way their grain shows in slowly curving vertical lines on the trunk and branches, or how the trees twist and stretch out from their bases like a snapshot of a dancer mid-twirl. The only people I passed were an elderly couple right near the

Juniper tree at Escalante Petrified Forest State Park.

trailhead. The transition from the main trail onto the Trail of Sleeping Rainbows (an unbelievably fitting name) found me immersed in fragments of petrified trees. Roughhewn geometric chunks of rainbow polished smooth, strands of orange, red, yellow and the deepest purple I may have ever seen, surrounded me.

However, none of this beauty seems to be what people remember about Escalante. Rather, it's the curse. It would seem that Escalante has a supernatural partner who enforces the old "take only memories, leave only footprints" adage. For at least four park managers' tenures (a timeline potentially spanning back pre-internet), rangers at Escalante have received packages containing pieces of petrified wood and letters detailing the cursed luck the thief had since they pocketed their prize. According to Bevan Monroe, the current park manager, "Depending on the season, we'll get one parcel every week....During the slower season, like the last couple months, we've actually only had, maybe, one box a month." If we extrapolate that over the past managers' tenures (let's assume each tenure lasts about ten years, not unrealistic for an upper-tier position), that comes out to around 1,200 packages. That seems a not altogether inconsequential number. And even if the amount and consistency of returns doesn't prove the reality of the curse—correlation is not causation, volume of believers does not equal validity of belief, etc.—it does prove that the idea of the curse has stuck with us, becoming a part of our collective culture in a unique and important way. Is it our social consciousness that keeps the legend of the curse alive? Is it some shared guilt over the manner in which our westward expansion has changed, often for the worse, the face of nature? Could it even tie into the fear so many Americans feel about the things that were done to ensure that westward expansion, things we are collectively uncomfortable enough about that we've all but removed mention of them from school curricula?

In some of the more mundane letters, small children—I imagine under the gaze of reprimanding parents—apologize for the theft, acknowledging that they "knew better." One letter written in a child's scratches on a Golden Nugget Casino notepad reads:

> *Dear, park rangers i took a piece of petrified wood I donot want bad luck im sorry. Sam.*
> *P.s. I picked it up on the trail if you want to put it back.*

Some of the pieces don't take long at all to return. Their temporary owners cite weeks or months of bad luck as the impetus for the return. Others get returned only after reflection has led the owner to place responsibility for years or decades of bad luck on the colorful little block. As for the bad luck people experience, well, that can range from ambiguous claims of "nothing has gone right" to a more macabre account placing responsibility for the death of a loved one on the forest's now infamous curse. In a typed letter, Kaspar Rudisuhli from Switzerland states:

> *By this letter I am restituting after examination 3 small pieces of Petrified Wood found in the region of Escalante State Park. I think they should belong to the Petrified Forest Museum. Remembering the warning in your famous Museum I acknowledge that since my travel 3 years ago I had no good luck in my life, but every year an accident or a disease, as other people had, too. I hope with this act of restitution Lord will have mercy upon me. I apologize and beg your pardon—sorry.*

Rudisuhli seems sincere in his desire for his bad luck to end. That the piece of petrified wood, and the curse, made it across the ocean before coming back speaks to the reach of Escalante's lore. In similar letters, people like Sabine from Germany say, "I had a lot of bad luck ever since then"; an anonymous writer says, "Things have just seemed off." These vague claims match the way we often look at things like good or bad luck. Our own confirmation bias grabs every small misfortune or bad day as evidence of bad luck resulting from a broken mirror or a black cat, a tipped-over salt shaker or a stroll under a ladder, while conveniently forgetting or minimizing our good days and happy accidents.

In a more specific and dramatic example, again from an unnamed writer, we find a Hollywood-worthy twist of irony.

> *I apologize for bringing these pieces of rock home. I wasn't aware of what they were until my brother in law told me the rules of the park. I just thought they were cool looking. I brought them back as a present for my brother—he's really into rocks.*
>
> *Not being one to believe in curses, but it's hard to explain the weird stuff that has happened since we got back—namely the unexpected death of the brother they were intended for.*
>
> *YOU CAN HAVE THEM BACK! I CERTAINLY DON'T WANT THEM ANYMORE. Thought of giving them to my ex sister in law but that wouldn't be very nice no matter how much I hate her.*

While the tone doesn't seem to fit a letter detailing the death of a loved one, the letter does provide more details than the average return note. Another difference between this and the typical letter is that the writer doesn't seem to show much remorse for the act of theft itself. Whereas many letters contain phrases like "please forgive me," "please accept our most sincere apologize," "I hope the spirit of the trees can now be at peace in their rightful place" and, of course the heartfelt "it was a crappy thing to do," this letter practically shoves the stones into the rangers' hands, shouting, "YOU CAN HAVE THEM BACK!"

I asked the park manager, Bevan, if he knew when people started talking about the curse and if there were stories about its origins. In my mind, I'd imagined high schoolers sharing campfire stories about a Native American chief placing a curse on the land or the curse resulting from some bloody battle between settlers and Natives. While this was not a far-fetched guess—the amount of supernatural lore with origin stories based on angry Natives is telling—it wasn't what Bevan had heard. What he had actually heard was nothing. In response to my question, he just shrugged his shoulders and said, "That I couldn't tell you. At least three park

Blocks of petrified wood at Escalante Petrified Forest State Park.

managers back, they all had the same kinda stories of things coming back and people having issues." One of Bevan's predecessors started displaying some of the letters. If you go into the visitor center, you can see them and their accompanying blocks of petrified wood in a large glass display box. As for the blocks of petrified wood that don't end up under glass? "I do the best I can to get them back out there," Bevan told me.

After my talk with Bevan, as I walked among the piñon and juniper trees, leftover rain clouds slowly gathered together, threatening another day of storms. It struck me how silent this place was, as if in its mystical slowing of time, sound, too, had been diffused. Occasionally a lone bird would sing out, but pauses weighed heavy in the gaps. Sitting on a large stone to take in my surroundings, I felt misplaced. I felt like a ghost in a house that was no longer theirs. Only this house was never mine, never ours, not really, not even now. I had hoped Bevan might provide me with a backstory, some narrative to help my mind close the chapter on Escalante, something that wrapped up the curse, the letters and the cultural implications with some insight into our past. What I was left with instead was this nothing, this silence, the way you can feel history like gravity in Escalante, and I was left with the thought that even though—and perhaps in part because—the forest has been here so long before us and because it will, hopefully, still be here long after us, we

Closeup of juniper tree at Escalante Petrified Forest State Park.

are the transient, incorporeal beings moving too fast through our hurried lives to appear as anything more than a blur in the corner of the world's eye. Our actions and our inability to think outside of a timeline that doesn't include us, as individuals and as a species, are the curse. We haunt this place, unwelcome visitors who occasionally make their presence and their power known. We are the poltergeists unnaturally moving things about and, yes, making some objects disappear.

CHAPTER 4

THE HAUNTING OF THE ST. GEORGE TEMPLE?

It was on November 9, 1871, in harsh desert conditions, beset by famine and frequent conflict with the Indigenous peoples who already lived there, that Brigham Young, second president of the Church of Jesus Christ of Latter-day Saints (LDS), better known as the Mormon church, announced that the first temple since the church had left Nauvoo, Illinois, would be built in St. George. Now, the temple stands out against the red rocks of the area, a white citadel in the center of sprawling suburbia. Its rounded dome tower—not the shorter original tower, which was struck by lightning—is one of the few LDS temple steeples that aren't topped with the iconic golden statue of the angel Moroni blowing his trumpet at the sky. There are a handful of curious stories about the building of the temple—from accounts of Young receiving revelation that the location for the temple had actually been dedicated centuries before by the Nephites (the early Christians Mormons believe preceded and became the Native Americans) to the story that the cannon the pioneers used as a weight to pound the footings for the temple had once been used by Napoleon's army.[38] This isn't surprising. Any monumental historic event is bound to have folklore attached to it. Add to this the fact that the line between official doctrine and folk belief in the LDS faith is fairly blurry—as sociologist Richley Crapo notes, "Although Mormons view doctrine as flowing down from the church hierarchy to the members, the bulk of what Mormons think of as doctrine actually arises from the grass-roots level as members... construct a distinctive Mormon view of reality"[39]—and the land the St. George Temple is built on becomes a fertile plot for intriguing tales.

St. George LDS Temple and visitor center.

After the Mormons began digging the temple's foundation, they discovered marshy land. That they used a cannon to hammer the temple footings into this land is recorded fact. The story of the cannon's attachment to Napoleon however, at least according to the website for the temple's visitor center, is not. The truth is that Erastus Snow sent Jesse W. Crosby to buy a cannon in California. Later, when it served no other purpose, the cannon was filled with lead and hoisted by rope and pulley, then dropped over and over again to hammer in the lava rock used to firm up the temple's foundation.

As for Young's revelation that the temple's location had been dedicated centuries before, we have only the word of David Henry Cannon Jr., one of the earliest settlers in the area. Cannon quotes Young as saying, upon discovery of the boggy undersoil, "We cannot move the foundation. This spot was dedicated by the Nephites. They could not build it (the temple), but we can and will build it for them."[40]

Temples are the most sacred places on earth for members of the LDS church. Mormons believe that inside of temples, they stand closer to heaven, "where God or other heavenly messengers can literally appear."[41] Because of the sacred nature of the ceremonies that take place inside of temples, Mormons are discouraged from sharing them with nonbelievers. This has led to some cultural conflict between the notions of secret and sacred.

In the lower levels of LDS temples, you'll find impressive-looking baptismal fonts, which are used exclusively for vicarious baptisms for the dead (the living are baptized in local church houses). These temple fonts are large, elevated stone pools that sit on the backs of twelve stone oxen representing the twelve tribes of Israel. Moving up the floors of the temple, you pass the lobby and changing rooms. Above, there are the endowment rooms. It is in these rooms that Mormons participate in their most sacred rituals, after which they enter the celestial room. Grand rooms dripping in opulence, celestial rooms are meant to be heaven on earth. Other notable rooms in temples are the sealing rooms (where marriages are performed), various council rooms for church leaders, and the holy of holies. According to current apostle Boyd K. Packer, the holy of holies "is where the president of the Church may retire when burdened down with heavy decisions to seek an interview with Him whose Church it is. The prophet holds the keys, the spiritual keys and the very literal key to this one door in that sacred edifice."[42] While only the Salt Lake Temple has an actual room called the holy of holies, every temple has sealing rooms that can be used as a holy of holies should church leadership need one.[43]

While not in the holy of holies, it was in the St. George Temple in August 1877 that fifty-four signers of the Declaration of Independence appeared to Wilford Woodruff, the future fourth president of the LDS church. The signers (minus John Hancock and William Floyd, who had already had their endowment ceremonies performed vicariously) appeared to Woodruff in a vision and argued—or demanded—that their endowments be done. "You have had the use of the Endowment House for a number of years and yet nothing has ever been done for us."[44] As the thirteenth president of the church (and fifteenth U.S. secretary of agriculture), Ezra Taft Benson, would later put it, "Think of it, the Founding Fathers of this nation, those great men, appeared within those walls and had their vicarious work done for them." The work didn't include only the signers of the declaration. Woodruff also performed vicarious ordinances for forty-four other "eminent men," including Benjamin Franklin, John Wesley and—perhaps a bit uncomfortably for contemporary Mormons, given modern society's opinion of him—Christopher Columbus.

This type of visitation is difficult to classify. Can we call spiritual encounters supernatural when they take place within a religious context? What makes one event spooky and another holy? Thomas Jefferson appearing to someone fifty-one years after his death seems hard to label as anything other than a ghost story, but to many people, when the event takes place within, as

Benson puts it, "sacred walls," calling it a ghost story is not just off-putting but bluntly offensive.

Whatever you call them—ghostly encounters or heavenly visitations—the supernatural events said to take place within temple walls aren't reserved just for prophets. Angels, loved ones, even God and Jesus can appear to any member of the church within the temple. It is a piece of LDS belief common enough that most of the people I talked to were well aware of it and had heard many versions of it but couldn't recall a specific story. This isn't uncommon with what folklorists call FOAF or Friend of a Friend stories,[45] those stories pervasive enough that you know you heard it but can't remember exactly where or from whom. However, two specific stories do stand out to me.

The first story was told to me by a former student during my time teaching at Utah Tech University (formerly Dixie State University). While discussing a personal essay in which the student was questioning her faith, she related to me that she had once been visited by Jesus in the celestial room. This was a returning student, probably in her fifties, and she struggled with an excess of guilt over doubting her faith. How could she doubt the "truth" of the church when she had literally seen Jesus in the temple? This is a unique example for several reasons. First, while I have had a dozen or so people throughout my life tell me that they saw Jesus, this woman was among the few who were sober and appeared to be of sound mind at the time that they told me. She seemed analytical, even skeptical. There is a notion, especially in academic circles, that supernatural beliefs and experiences are opposite to and void of rational, modern thought. However, as folklorist Diane E. Goldstein notes:

> *Recent phenomenological approaches to belief have...opposed traditional academic assumptions that supernatural belief traditions necessarily arise from various kinds of error. These studies demonstrate that careful analysis of belief traditions reveal reasoned consideration and the testing of alternatives on the part of percipients and narrators.*[46]

While most heavenly visitations are positive, even transformative, experiences, this experience, whatever it had once been for this student, had become a stone, increasing the weight of guilt associated with her religious doubt.

Likewise, the second story, related to me by the wife of a colleague, carries a feeling of discomfort. Mika can't recall the first time she saw a spirit, but she sees them all the time, so much so that she has become the go-to source for her friends and family when it comes to interactions with the other side. For them the question "Who you gonna call?" has a more personal and direct answer. Mika says that most of the spirits she sees aren't evil; rather, they're just sort of there, killing time. However, at times, even mundane spirits can become troublesome in large numbers. This is one reason Mika struggled with the temple. She recalls sitting in the celestial room of the St. George Temple and feeling smothered by all the spirits that filled the space. Even though the spirits seemed overjoyed to be there, the feeling started to overwhelm her, and Mika politely told her husband, "We need to go; it's getting too crowded in here." While many stories about spiritual visitors take place inside the temple, there are also those otherworldly occurrences that people have witnessed from outside of the temple.

There is an interesting dynamic within communities that have an LDS temple. Temples are large, beautiful but imposing structures that tend to seem like they're looming over a town if you are not a member of the LDS faith. Despite the church hosting public open houses before the dedication of each new temple, there can still be an air of strong separation or even othering in a community where only some people are allowed in the most prominent building in town. It is not unlike what folklorist Sylvia Ann Grider notes about the stereotypical Victorian-looking haunted house so common in American folklore. "What went on inside these mansions was the subject of much speculation by the general public. Since these were the dwellings of the super-rich, most Americans never set foot inside these mansions, which gave the buildings a sort of other-worldliness, anonymity, and mystery analogous to that of ruined European castles."[47] As many of the "non-Mormons" I spoke to noted, looking at the temple from the outside in can cause feelings of secrecy, division and exclusion.

Among those who aren't affiliated with the LDS church, there are different stories that surround the St. George Temple. Ghostly apparitions appear late at night in temple windows. Strange sounds emanate from the temple grounds during the witching hour. Some of these stories are ambiguous in their attitude toward the faith and organization associated with the temple; however, some express the cultural tension that can be felt between those on the outside and those on the inside.

Former southern Utah resident (and former Mormon) Jayme Fenn related several "outside the temple" stories to me.

> *There are spirits that roam the halls....You can see them at night in the second story windows....And when I was young doing baptism for the dead*

St. George LDS Temple by full moon.

> *there were 3 lil native kids trapped in the baptism room because they didn't want to be baptized because they would not be with their families, so they are stuck in the temple not able to pass because of the Mormon religion trapping their souls with their baptism....So they forever roam the basement of the temple...and when I was there they were outside the pool of water crying begging to go home.*

To say that the relationship between the LDS pioneers who settled Utah and the Indigenous peoples who already occupied the area was complicated is a gross oversimplification, even if a more locally acceptable one. Hundreds of skirmishes were recorded between the pioneers and the Natives. Forts dot the state from south to north in testament to them. But beyond the battlefield, the relationship between these groups is a tangle of slavery and deracination. The Native American slave trade was thriving before the Mormons made their way west. Traffic in Natives was already booming in New Mexico thanks to the Spanish expansion to the north. Michael Bennion notes in *Captivity, Adoption, Marriage, and Identity: Native American Children in Mormon Homes*:

> *As Spanish influence extended north into the Great Basin of present-day Utah and Nevada, ancient Indian servitude patterns, based on tribal assimilation and repopulation, combined in new and disturbing ways with the Spanish need for forced labor to make a profound mark on the culture of Southwest slavery. Utes, Comanches and others developed an aggressive, slave-oriented, raid-and-trade political economy based on the horses and guns acquired from Europeans.*

The Mormon pioneers—who had brought a number of Black slaves with them on the trip west—fell right into this slave trade once they settled in the Salt Lake Valley. The LDS Church (and thus the territory of Utah) formally legalized slavery with the Act in Relation to Service on February 4, 1852. The law largely centered on the treatment of Black slaves and punishment for miscegenation—mixing of the races. The day after passing the act, Brigham Young elaborated upon his stance on slavery:

> *I am as much opposed to the principle of slavery as any man in the present acceptation or usage of the term. It is abused. I am opposed to abusing that which God decreed, to take a blessing and make a curse of it. It is a great blessing to the seed of Adam to have the seed of Cain*

> *(African Americans) as servants, but those they serve should use them with all…heart and feeling.*[48]

A month later, Young followed up on the Act in Relation to Service with the Act for the Relief of Indian Slaves and Prisoners, which primarily dealt with the proper treatment of Native slaves. While this act did provide protections for Indigenous slaves and is phrased as if it is an act of kindness to them, it still positioned the Mormons as superior not only to the Natives but also to the Mexican slave owners, whom Young noted were "scarcely superior"[49] to the Natives.

Depending on your stance in relation to the LDS church, it is easy to either present these actions as a prophet of God leading his people in a small step toward equality by passing laws that encouraged members of the church to purchase Native slaves as well as educate and enculturate them—or as the story of a conquering people dealing with what they see as an inferior race by means of slavery and cultural genocide.

These differences in cultural perspective are deep seated and thus find their way into our folklore, where we are often more comfortable expressing such things. Cultural tension about the LDS practice of baptisms for the dead (vicarious baptism) and the treatment or mistreatment of Indigenous peoples often sit just beneath the surface of coworker relations, extended family dinners, even classroom discussions. That stories like Jayme's about the crying Native children exist speaks to that tension. However, not all numinous stories about the temple fall so clearly on one side or the other.

One ambiguous, perhaps bending toward positive, story from outside the temple comes from Jennifer Brown Bennet. It was late fall 1991, just after eleven o'clock at night, and Jennifer was driving home from a friend's house.

> *On the top floor* [of the Temple] *I saw a glowing shaped person in the top main floor window. They stayed there for what seemed like forever. I drove around the building and came around to the side again, thinking that maybe I was seeing things. But, sure enough, it was still there. I was creeped out sorta but just left.*

I asked Jennifer if she could still picture the glowing person she saw.

> *From the ground, you see a shape of a human. Almost looking out, who's trapped. I had the feeling it was there like it was guarding. Like it wasn't free to wander. The glowing person looked like a woman to me. In white.*

> *Somewhat like what you'd expect someone in the temple would look like. Long-sleeved dress in white, and her hair and body glowed similarly to her dress. Her hair was loose around her shoulders, on the longer side. Her dress came up to her neck like an 1800s style. Her hair was not blonde, grey, brown or black. It glowed like a lightbulb gold. While she seemed beautiful and standing guard, I felt she wanted to see other things. She seemed humble and accepted her charge. But as she stood looking out, I felt her presence.*

Jennifer added,

> *I knew nobody should be inside since my father was a temple worker. He told stories, too, of the holy of holies. That when he'd get inside in the mornings on a first shift of the day...that they were instructed to not enter that room if they saw a light from under the door. This was between 1992–1999. When he was a temple worker. That room is the uppermost chamber in the temple. Very few are allowed there.*

Jennifer's story is interesting in part because it has elements of the outside and inside the temple perspective. The glowing figure is a humble guardian with a holy charge and yet still someone who "creeped out" Jennifer. Members of the church hesitate to share memorate like Jennifer's for several reasons. First, like anyone with a memorate, LDS or not, they may be concerned that people will think that either they made it up or they're crazy. But the reasons multiply when your memorate could border on the heretical. As an author simply identified as Your Mormon Auntie wrote in an article about Mormons and the supernatural for a local paper, "Mormons tend to stray away from the believing side of this sort of thing....This could be part of our LDS reluctance to acknowledge non-churchy interactions with the spirit world: Maybe we think that if people doubt our ghost experiences, they'll be more likely to doubt our Holy Ghost experiences."[50] The blurring between ghost and holy ghost, along with the gray area between "official doctrine" and "grassroots beliefs" that Crapo noted, can create strain for those Mormons who experience memorate, even if the event is religious in nature. As Eric A. Eliason noted in discussing Mormon folklore of pre-birth experiences (PBEs):

> *Positive valuation of "faith-promoting rumors" such as PBEs coexist with caution toward them. Sharing such stories may make one seem kooky, even to other Mormons. Merciless internet debunkings can reveal one as a dupe,*

The upper windows of the Thomas Forsyth House, where Aaron would have seen the woman in white.

> *but being too skeptical of a friend's personal experience can brand one insensitive to spiritual things. Perhaps in a community open to visions, miracles, and prophecies it is especially important to guard against fakery. But Salt Lake City has no office like the Vatican's that investigates miracles and pronounces them genuine or fraudulent; Mormons are generally on their own in such matters. Many Mormons avoid giving too much credence to such tales the further away they get from first hand experience. And some first hand experiences are accompanied by an impression not to share them except in sacred moments.*[51]

Keeping this in mind, I asked Jennifer if she ever shared her "ghost experience" with her temple worker father.

> *Yes. He said he's seen and heard many things. Whispers from that top room. Loads of things like that. He said he believed me. He'd had his own experiences. I will say that none of them were bad experiences. All*

> *strange, interesting, and good. Nothing like something chasing you down a hall or anything.*

It is tempting to build from Jennifer's story and say that the difference between the spooky and the holy is the nature of the experience, positive or negative. As Mika told me, "I don't call the good spirits hauntings." But what do we do then with something like Aaron Timm's story from chapter 1? If we framed Aaron's story in scripture, would it change the way we look at it? Would it increase its cultural value? And should it? It was, by her own account, a positive experience, something that helped her—a young girl struggling with feelings of isolation—to feel less alone. In sharing Aaron's story with people, I've found most of them respond positively. They see how much the story might have meant to a young woman, and through that empathy, they are able to move the story from something they'd simply categorize as a campfire ghost story to something they might share with a bit more reverence. Is empathy, then, the key to bridging some of the cultural gaps these stories highlight? Non-Mormon to Mormon? Majority to minority? Ghost story to holy ghost story?

CHAPTER 5

ROUTE 666

The Devil's Highway

It was a dark and stormy night...but no, it really was. If I had checked weather predictions for weeks, I couldn't have picked a better night for a drive on historic Route 666—the devil's highway. Rain tapped on my windshield at a steady pace, and lightning flashed in the distance, filling the sky every minute or so with brilliant white light.

The route, renamed Route 491 piece by piece from 1985 to 2003, stretches from Gallup, New Mexico, to Monticello, Utah. Originally a branch off of U.S. Route 66, 491 runs through New Mexico, Arizona (though that portion has been renumbered to be part of U.S. 191), Utah and the tribal lands of both the Navajo Nation and the Ute Mountain Ute Tribes. The stretch of highway goes through the breathtaking desert of the Four Corners area, where flat land stretches off into the distance, a silence punctuated only by majestic stone formations—mesas, mountains and bluffs reaching toward a broad sky. Route 491 also passes multiple sites sacred to the Indigenous peoples of the area, among them two mountains: Sleeping Ute Mountain (Wisuv Káruv to the Ute and Dził Naajiní to the Navajo) and Shiprock (Tsé Bit'a'í or "rock with wings" in Navajo).

Several groups made separate attempts to rename the road, largely due to the connotation of its name with the Christian concept of the number of the beast (as found in the book of Revelations), though sign theft was also cited by some as a reason to

Opposite: Graphic of a sign for U.S. Route 666. *Pixabay*.

Above: The current name for U.S. Route 666 (U.S. Route 491).

make the change. U.S. 666 stretched through sacred land for decades before its renumbering. Even now, despite the renumbering to 491, the stigma of 666 stays with the highway. Urban legends containing a variety of demonic goings-on cling to the road, but if we look beyond the lore—which we can debate the veracity of all day long—there is an evil based in facts and details that are all too real.

The naming of the road is actually far more bureaucratic than satanic. According to a Federal Highway Administration report by Richard F. Weingroff, the number for the famous Route 66 was actually supposed to be 60; thus, Route 666 would have been Route 660.

> *Following complaints from Kentucky and other States in the East that "60" should have been assigned to a transcontinental route through their States, the number "60" became the subject of the most protracted and bitter controversy involving the numbering plan. The compromise solution was to assign "60" to a route from Virginia Beach, Virginia to Springfield, Missouri, and "66" to the Chicago-to-Los Angeles route.... The change to "66" meant that the former branches of "60" had to be renumbered as branches of the new number.*[52]

The route itself is a treacherous one and was even more treacherous before safety improvements were made in recent years, the latest of which occurred in 2014.[53] As an article from the *Roosevelt Review* notes, "In just a 60 mile stretch of the highway, there are approximately 400 sharp curves. In fact, in 1997 the Route 666 was determined to be one of the most hazardous roads in the nation."[54] This sentiment was also felt by travel writer James T. Yenckel, who added:

> *An almost empty highway to nowhere, U.S. 666 climbs to above 9,000 feet along the Coronado Trail in a cliff-hanging series of twists and turns so sharp the speed limit often drops to 10 miles per hour. The reward for this little test of nerves is a picture-postcard panorama of pine-draped ridges leap-frogging the horizon.*[55]

For many people, it would seem that placing the blame for the accidents on the road's association with the Christian devil made more sense than pointing to poor planning. Whether it was the thought of a cursed road or the accident statistics that kept people from using 666 is unsure (though local politicians felt that the association with the number of the beast certainly kept travelers and their money from passing through the area).[56]

At the time of the road's final renaming in 2003, *New York Times* journalist Jodi Wilgoren took her own trip along the devil's highway. While many of the locals she spoke to felt the whole situation was much ado about nothing (including several business owners who felt the name had no impact on the local economy), a handful of residents did have stories to share:

> *"I've lost so many relatives on this road," said Joe Hulligan, who sells bowls, mugs and vases at the Ute Mountain Reservation pottery shop, in Towaoc, Colo.... "They were going around that corner, and they just went too fast."*
>
> *At the Ute tribe's casino, where 6-6-6, like any three of a kind, pays 30 to 1 in three-card poker, the dealers each had bad-luck stories. Harold Graves said he found a dead man hanging from a tree in front of his house on the highway about a year ago.*
>
> *Charlie Lanford's girlfriend was killed on Route 666 four years back. "The Devil," Mr. Lanford explained, "and the tequila."*[57]

While urban legends of devil dogs and demon trucks cling to the curving highway, stories steeped in Indigenous spirituality pull up close to the land it cuts through. One of the two sacred mountains that U.S. 666 passes, Sleeping Ute Mountain, is said to resemble a Ute chief sleeping on his back with his arms folded across his chest. The mountain range is also a vital site in certain Ute ceremonies. The U.S. government took the land from the Utes in a series of early treaties, and the tribe had to buy it back in 1911 by giving the government some of the land that is now part of Mesa Verde National Park. To most non-Native people, this type of information is historical minutiae. But for the Ute Mountain Ute Tribe, it meant they could control access to an area they see as sacred. And that sounds nice; it wraps up a complicated moment in history with a tidy bow. However, it isn't an entirely accurate representation of how things went down. The Mesa Verde land trade was less an instance of the government allowing the Utes to buy something special back and more another example of the United States giving a token in exchange as they took whatever they wanted. As chief negotiator for the Bureau of Indian Affairs Frederick Abbott told the Utes during the 1911 negotiation:

> *The government is stronger than the Utes.... When the government finds old ruins on land that it wants to take for public purposes, it has the right to take it.... The government is strong enough to take land away from the Ute Indians that it wants for a National Park.... Congress is going to have that land.*[58]

As is so frequently and dishearteningly the case with U.S. government and Native relations, the government was going to get what it wanted by coercion, force or deception—Indigenous rights be damned. The real kicker here is that, as National Park superintendent Jesse L. Nusbaum would eventually admit, the Utes already had the rights to the Ute Mountain lands the government sold them in exchange for the Mesa Verde land. If this moment in history is to be wrapped up in a bow, it's an ugly one: the U.S. government forced the Utes to give them roughly ten thousand acres of land and in turn paid them with a lie.

The tribal story associated with Sleeping Ute Mountain is also quite poignant given the modern context:

> *In the very old days, the Sleeping Ute Mountain was a Great Warrior God. He came to help fight against the Evil Ones who were causing much trouble. A tremendous battle between the Great Warrior God and the Evil Ones followed. As they stepped hard upon the earth and braced themselves*

to fight, their feet pushed the land into mountains and valleys. This is how the country of this region came to be as it is today. The Great Warrior God was hurt, so he lay down to rest and fell into a deep sleep. The blood from his wound turned into living water for all creatures to drink. When the fog or clouds settle over the Sleeping Warrior God, it is a sign that he is changing his blankets for the four seasons. When the Indians see the light green blanket over their "God," they know it is spring. The dark green blanket is summer, the yellow and red one is fall, and the white one is winter. The Indians believe that when the clouds gather on the highest peak, the Warrior God is pleased with his people and is letting rain clouds slip from his pockets. They also believe that the Great Warrior God will rise again to help them in the fight against their enemies.[59]

Though it is referencing events well before colonial times, the story of the battle between the Great Warrior God and the Evil Ones feels like it could as well be describing the events of early American history with the "Evil Ones" causing much trouble: creating unethical treaties and then breaking those treaties, slaughtering innocents, kidnapping children and forcing them to abandon and ignore their heritage and religion. You know, trouble.

Sleeping Ute Mountain isn't the only mountain with a "sleeping" story attached to it. Mount Timpanogos, which sits in my hometown of American Fork, is said to hold the legend of a sleeping maiden, Utana, who, lost in despair at the death of her true love, Red Eagle, threw herself off the mountain. The famous heart-shaped stalactite in Timpanogos Cave is said to have been created by the Great Spirit merging the two lovers' hearts. The problem with this story is that it isn't Native in origin. According to a *Deseret News* article from 2010, "There is no evidence...that Timpanogos' legend is an authentic Native American Legend....It was mostly likely invented by Utah Valley resident Eugene Lusk Roberts, who promoted the mountain and started an annual hike to the summit of the mountain."[60] Eugene wasn't the first and certainly wouldn't be the last non-Native person to manipulate, create or straight-up steal Indigenous beliefs in an attempt to commodify the beliefs of a people who had already suffered so much at the hands of Western culture. From Hollywood's co-opting of skinwalkers and windingos to New Agers' use of crystals, sage and sweat lodges, there seems to always be a market for Native beliefs so long as they aren't presented by the hands of actual Native individuals. As Jackie Krogmeier notes in an article for the *Purdue Historian*, "New Agers participate amongst themselves (rarely do they interact with Native communities, or seek Native opinions) in their recreation of Native ceremonies and rituals, often purchasing items that hold relevance to Native religions, such as eagle feathers, pipes, and special stones."[61] While there is a monetary side to this issue—rarely does money for "Native" items make it into Native communities—we cannot ignore the social and emotional pain caused by seeing people participate in and profit from a culture that Natives had been derided and marginalized for, a culture and belief system that they themselves weren't legally allowed to practice in the United States until 1978.[62]

As for the other sacred mountain that sits along the devil's highway, Shiprock gained its name from pioneers who saw a resemblance between the mountain and the popular clipper ships of the time. Its native name, "rock with wings," however, fits the Navajo story of the mountain better. According to some Navajo beliefs, their ancestors were brought to the land from the north by a great bird, thus the rock with wings. But Shiprock also ties into a handful of other Native stories and ceremonies, including but not limited to the Enemy Side Ceremony, the Navajo Mountain Chant, the Bead Chant and the Naayee'ee Ceremony. [63] Indigenous beliefs are beautiful and complex, and honestly, they can be confusing to even well-intentioned

Shiprock. *Pixabay.*

outsiders. To really grasp the beliefs of any of the over 120 different Native tribes requires a hard paradigm shift. These are belief systems that were built on a completely different understanding of and approach to reality than most of us were raised with. They are also beliefs that the U.S. government put great effort into erasing. As Krogmeier notes:

> *The appropriation of Native culture is particularly painful to Native Americans because of how stigmatized and oppressed their own practice of it has been in our history, and continues to be. For a non-Native to take what has been stolen from Native Americans so lightly is offensive, and damaging to Native efforts to re-educate their people in the correct, reverent ways of their culture.*[64]

How often do we, speaking here to non-Natives, inadvertently hinder Native efforts to reclaim a culture previous generations stole from them? How often do we perpetuate stereotypes and misunderstandings that make their path more difficult? How often do we continue the theft of that culture?

Non-Native cultures aren't barren of lore, either. From the non-Native side of the story, tales range from demon truckers driving people off the road to hellhounds chasing cars and ghostly hitchhikers appearing and then disappearing.[65] Though I've only heard them from non-Native people, many stories include the Navajo legend of skinwalkers (I discuss skinwalkers in depth in chapter 10). Some of these stories connect to broader urban legends, like the young woman stranded on the side of the road in a white nightgown who either disappears when you stop to help or will suddenly appear in the backseat of your car if you don't stop to help. This is one of many versions of the popular vanishing hitchhiker urban legend.

Further along my midnight drive of Route 666, the weather had calmed only slightly. Lights skirted the edge of the road, but the tail of the storm had diffused those lights in the distance, creating an eerily glowing mist sitting just at the edge of my horizon. I'd kept my eyes peeled but hadn't seen a hellhound or a ghostly hitchhiker. My air conditioning brought in the heavy, refreshing scent of rain as another big rig screamed past me. While Route 666 does have lore of demon truckers and ghost trucks running drivers off the road, and while there did seem to be a higher-than-normal number of semis on this route, I'd yet to see a semi with unnatural red lights and, to both my disappointment and my relief, none of them tried to run me off of the road. Linda Dunning, whose book *Lost Landscapes* is filled with questionable research and a weighty lack of citations, tells her husband's experience with

U.S. Route 491 during the author's midnight drive.

one ghost truck on the devil's highway. According to Dunning, one night, while heading to Gallop on Route 666, he saw something off in the distance:

> *He was alone and hadn't seen a car for miles and miles. Suddenly, he saw a truck that looked like it was on fire heading straight for him, right down the middle of the highway. The large truck was going so fast that sparks were flying up off the wheels and flames were coming from the smokestack....He estimated that the truck was going 130 miles an hour.*[66]

The event terrified Dunning's husband, and he pulled off to the side of the road, ran a bit into the desert and waited for the truck to pass.

Of all the things that a demon can possess, there may be nothing more American than a demon automobile. From Stephen King's (and John Carpenter's) *Christine* and the 1986 film *Maximum Overdrive* to urban legends about James Dean's haunted Porsche 550, "Little Bastard," American identity has long been tied to our cars, so it's not surprising that American pop culture is filled with examples of that connection going horribly wrong. Automobiles—and the open road, for that matter—represent freedom, embracing risks and establishing status. Sometimes, though, the status is hollow, the risk is not worth the price and the freedom too often comes with consequences for others. Supernatural lore about possessed vehicles can represent all of these things, as well as the excesses of commercialism and industrialization.

While we might own the market when it comes to demonic autos, America is the new kid on the block when it comes to demons in general. The world's cultures are filled with a colorful spectrum of "demons." From the Greek daimons, which were not evil but rather somewhat ambiguous spirits of divine power,[67] to the ancient Mesopotamian "offspring of Arali," who would escape the underworld to terrorize mortals on earth,[68] to Indra and Ahriman, the malicious deities of the Vedic texts,[69] the history of demons is a wash of one culture or religion influencing another. The Christian concept of demons can itself be traced back to Zoroastrianism.[70] Before that—specifically, before the Hebrew was translated into Greek—*demon* was a label for the "Gods of other Nations" in what is now called the Old Testament.[71] The modern idea of Christian demonology—those beings of pure evil who love nothing more than to possess humans—comes from the "legion" of the New Testament that Jesus cast out of the man and into the swine. It also comes from popular media: the horror genre with its exorcisms and possessions, its cults summoning demons and its new age spiritualists who evict demonic spirits from haunted homes. Could a highway, simply because of its incidental association with an "evil" number, become haunted, possessed or cursed? Of course, that begs the question of whether demons and evil, in the absolute religious sense, exist. But for now, it is enough to discuss that a significant portion of us (41%) believe these things exist, and regardless of whether you or I believe in them, they have become a part of our cultural fabric.[72]

The number 666 gains its association with evil from the book of Revelation. In chapter 13, verses 16–18 of the King James Version of the Bible, it says:

> *And he causeth all, both small and great, rich and poor, free and bond, to receive a mark in their right hand, or in their foreheads: / And that no man might buy or sell, save he that had the mark, or the name of the beast, or the number of his name. / Here is wisdom. Let him that hath understanding count the number of the beast: for it is the number of a man; and his number is six hundred threescore and six.*

Threescore is 3 x 20, or 60, thus the Number of the Beast (in the common understanding, the devil's number) is 666. The number has woven itself into pop culture. Films like *666 the Beast*, *666 the Child* and the Lou Diamond

Phillips film *Route 666* directly reference the number in their titles, but dozens more play with or reference the idea: the *Omen* franchise, *Pulp Fiction* and *The Phantom of the Opera*, among others.

Public consciousness is usually crafted by a mix of popular culture and prominent religion. So, whether it's the biblical understanding of 666 as the Number of the Beast or mass media's commodification of it that has had more social influence is difficult to discern. Still, the overall impact is easily documented. From personal examples (your aunt Karen who warns you about *Harry Potter* because of some weird math connecting the letters in J.K. Rowling's name to 666) to examples of more national and even international interest, you can find the Number of the Beast everywhere. Former first lady Nancy Reagan refused to have her Los Angeles address include 666; it was instead changed to 668 St. Cloud Road. In 2006, a rash of women across the globe worried about giving birth on June 6.[73] More recently, some religious extremists leaned into the anti-vax movement by connecting the COVID-19 vaccines with the Number of the Beast. And one of Salt Lake City's most notable urban legends, the grave of Lilly E. Gray, centers on the inscription at the bottom of her grave, which reads, "Victim of the Beast 666."

However, this number might not be a correct translation of the original text. The oldest living version of the Book of Revelation, Papyrus 115, lists the number as 616, not 666. This is a notable discrepancy that is also present in the Codex Ephraemi Rescriptus.[74] In fact, many textual criticism scholars, including Eberhard Nestle and Kurt Aland, have stated that 666 is actually the textual variant of the more correct 616.[75]

What, then, can we make of this mingling of cultures and histories, beliefs and theology? Two cultures, the Navajo and the Ute, cherish a beautiful land of color for its connection to their history, their stories and their beliefs. A newer culture—that is itself a curious mix of past cultures—brought its fear of the dark into that land. Westward expansion and, essentially, colonization have cut asphalt lines through the lands and beliefs of the Navajo and Ute. A black mark, of the beast or not, runs through the Four Corners area. As we drive along it and the other U.S. highways, as we visit beautiful national parks built on questionable grounds, as we examine where our pride, fears and sense of identity lie, it's worth learning from the hard facts that surround the lore. It's worth looking beyond the shiny packaging that some of our stories come in to take in the darker elements; because if the devils are in the details, then the greatest trick they ever pulled truly was convincing us they didn't exist…or matter.

CHAPTER 6

KEEPING THE DEAD ALIVE

The Interesting Case of Lydia Knight

It was just after midnight as I crept through the St. George cemetery, dark enough that I'd have tripped without the light on my cell phone. I'd come to capture a picture of a specific headstone set against a full moon and an eerily cloudy night sky. The headstone, a large—by far the largest in this cemetery—granite orb set on a geometric base, belongs to Lydia Knight, purchased for her by her son Jesse Knight, a wealthy silver capitalist toward the end of the 1800s. The cemetery's open hours ended a while ago, but as with most people who come to cemeteries for reasons other than visiting the graves of loved ones, my purpose better fit a late-night setting.

Lying on fresh-cut grass, I tried to balance my camera for the extended exposure the photo would require (my tripod was still boxed up from our recent move). I've done extended exposure photos like this a handful of times, without a tripod, and it's always extra tricky. The slightest shift in a thirty-second exposure will obscure the subject, instead filling the frame with motion blur. If you're lucky, accidental motion blur can create an abstract atmospheric gem, but I was not there for abstract atmosphere. My hope, as always, was to create clarity and provide detail without sacrificing the atmosphere.

It's safe to say that the majority of the people who have visited Lydia's grave over the years have not come to pay tribute to Lydia but to experience the lore associated with her grave; namely, that if you visit her grave and perform any of several versions of the correct ritual (circling the grave a

The headstone of Lydia Knight by full moon.

certain number of times and saying the correct phrase a certain number of times), you will be able to hear Lydia speak. There is no mention in the lore of who Lydia was. Likewise, there is no reason given as to why it would be worth hearing *what* Lydia has to say. It's enough that she is dead, and typically, dead people don't speak.

For their final, students in the second semester of my Academic Approaches to the Supernatural class have to pick a supernatural claim of some kind to conduct an experiment on. The catch is that, unlike the overwhelming majority of "ghost hunters," their experiments must follow rigorous scientific methodology. One of my students chose to do her final on the lore surrounding Lydia's grave. Her experiment involved six individuals taking turns walking around the gravestone at night. There were variables in the number of times they'd circle the grave and one subject who stood still. Some subjects also walked in the opposite direction. The participants then did the same thing in the daytime. Much to her satisfaction, and my disappointment (I'm always a little disappointed when the supernatural fails to show up), none of the subjects heard or recorded anything.

While most people who visit Lydia's grave, like my student, make only one trip, maybe two, Utah Tech University English professor Ami Comeford has been visiting Lydia Knight's grave since her childhood, not to test the lore but to visit the grave of a beloved ancestor. When I asked Ami what she thought of people legend tripping to Lydia's grave, she said, "It feels like it trivializes her life a little bit, and I'm not sure I'm super comfortable, certainly [not] in participating in it." Ami's sister, however, takes her nephews and nieces to Lydia's grave for Halloween, mixing local lore and personal heritage. Being able to balance both of those sides is something Ami said she admires in her sister.

The lore surrounding Lydia's grave could go back as far as the 1940s; regardless, it circulated prominently by the time Ami was in sixth grade or so. She recalls hearing kids talk about it on the bus ride to school, which went past the cemetery. "We would drive by the cemetery on the bus every day and it was always, 'Have you seen that gravestone? It says, 'Not dead but sleeping.''' As a child, little more than a disconnect existed between the grave she visited with her grandmother and mother every Memorial Day and the grave students talked about on the bus. It would be later, when she developed a stronger feeling of connection to Lydia, that Ami started to struggle with the lore.

This type of legend tripping based off of local lore is usually the terrain of high school students exploring their independence. As folklorists Lynne

Closeup of Lydia Knight's headstone, featuring the phrase "Not dead but sleeping."

S. McNeill and Elizabeth Tucker say in the introduction to their book *Legend Tripping*:

> *Carrying plenty of ghost-hunting equipment and steeling themselves to be brave no matter what happens, teens plunge into the realm of the supernatural. Their parents may raise hell if they find out where they've gone, and police may cause trouble if they notice the intrusion, but the kids accept these risks. Their trip is important; it helps them navigate the difficult passage from childhood to adulthood.*[76]

However, legend tripping is not exclusively teenagers' terrain. In fact, as ghost hunting has become more culturally acceptable through shows like *Ghost Hunters*, *Ghost Adventures* and *Buzzfeed Unsolved: Supernatural*, adults are finding their own spot in the world of legend tripping.

While Cyndee Spilker-Jacobson first heard the lore surrounding Lydia's grave as a child, it wasn't until her thirties that she organized an adventure to check it out. "The earliest and the only [version of the story], it was repeated by every local around, was that if you walked around the headstone three times calling out her name that she would appear." While the version Cyndee recalls is the most common, other versions of the lore hold that you should circle the headstone six times, and if you ask, "Lydia, Lydia, what do you hear?" you can hear her respond. Or that if you visit the grave on a full moon during the witching hour, you'll see it glow.

Cyndee decided to investigate the lore after discussing it with some of her nursing friends from work. Cyndee, her friend Emily and Emily's mother planned to make the trip, walk the circles and see if Lydia spoke or appeared. They'd also take a recording device to see if they could capture any EVP (electronic voice phenomenon—disembodied voices that you can hear only on the recording). However, the night of the adventure, the hospital called Cyndee in to work. Anxious to hear how it went, she spoke to Emily the next day, only to be informed that the adventure had been uneventful. Still, Cyndee, who has always felt a connection to the supernatural, wanted to hear the recording. So, later, sitting on Emily's couch, she pressed play. "I listen to it, and I hear very clearly, like plain as day, after they said, 'Lydia, are you here?,' right after they ask that, it was plain as day, it says 'I am right here.' Just like that, like a really heavy whisper." At first, Cyndee thought Emily had to be playing a prank on her: "I looked at her like, 'Oh, you guys are so funny.' I'm like, you guys whispered in the recorder." But Emily assured her that they hadn't and, after listening to it for herself, became quite scared. "It really freaked her out....Then we replayed it for her husband and her mom as well." Each person heard the same thing "plain as day." Is it important that the supernatural experience was sought after, not spontaneous? As folklorist Diane E. Goldstein notes, "The issue of induced or intentional versus spontaneous experience always makes academics uncomfortable. Going in search of an experience...appears always to be tinged with a sense of the artificial, a sense that participation is about the fulfillment of expectations."[77] In my class, we discuss this idea as I lecture about the difference between investigating "if" something is true versus "that" something is true. It is, in part, the difference between the mindsets Chet Raymo labels "skeptics and true believers."

The night I visited Lydia's headstone to snap my photo, as I walked along the lines of graves, I heard a noise. It could have been anything, but the timing coincided exactly with me losing my balance as I stepped on a fresh grave plot. I had come with the mindset of a photographer exploring somewhere they technically weren't supposed to be after hours. I was thinking about exposure, aperture and shutter speed, bokeh and the possibility of an encounter with the police. I was too focused on the technical aspects of why I'd come to jump to supernatural conclusions, but if I'd been there, alone at night, looking for the supernatural, might I have just found something? A distant, unexplained sound as I stepped on a fresh grave plot—could it have become a story I'd share around campfires someday? My experience with the supernatural? It was subtle, but most memorate are. As folklorist Jeannie Banks Thomas notes:

> *Ghost stories from the contemporary oral tradition are frequently only slightly dramatic. The drama comes from the subject matter and the manner in which people tell the stories rather than from the extraordinary behavior of the supernatural beings. In the oral tradition, people commonly report merely feeling some type of "presence," a cold feeling in the room, or strange noises and nothing more.*[78]

I ran into this "only *slightly* dramatic" idea time and again while gathering stories. So often, someone's big spooky story peaks at "we just felt a dark presence."

When Ami Comeford says that the lore, including strangers legend tripping to Lydia's grave, seems to minimize the life of a remarkable person, she's not just speaking for herself. In recent years, due to her connection to Joseph Smith and early church historical events, Lydia has become somewhat of a Latter-day Saint celebrity.

Lydia joined the Mormon church in Canada after her family sent her there to recover from a tumultuous first marriage to a "terrible drunkard." More than just a drunkard, Lydia's husband abused and abandoned her, newly with child, taking everything they had. Despite their concerns about her having joined this new religion, her family sent her to Kirtland with her inheritance to get a fresh start. Upon arriving at Kirtland, Lydia was greeted with the news that the Prophet Joseph Smith had again been imprisoned. As Vincent Knight told her:

> *Sister, the Prophet is in bondage and has been brought into distress by the persecutions of the wicked, and if you have any means to give, it will be a benefit to him." "Oh yes, sir," she replied, "here is all I have. I only wish it was more," emptying her purse, containing, perhaps fifty dollars, in his hand as she spoke. He looked at it and counted it and fervently exclaimed: "Thank God, this will release and set the Prophet free!"*[79]

Without money "even to procure a meal or a night's lodging" Lydia had no means with which to care for herself. In gratitude for what she had done, Vincent Knight and his wife welcomed her into their home, where she stayed for some time until, as Susa Gates's *Lydia Knight's History* states:

> *In the Fall of '35, the Prophet's brother Hyrum requested Lydia to come to his home and assist his wife. He promised her she should receive all the care and thought that could be given to her if she really were at home. She complied with the request, and while living there became acquainted with one of the brethren who boarded at the place while working on the Kirtland Temple. His name was Newel Knight, although not related in any way with the Knight family spoken of in the beginning of this chapter.*[80]

Newel immediately took notice of the young guest. And thus started what is now called "The Love Story of Nauvoo."

Like any good love story, there needs to be some conflict, something keeping the lovers apart. For Lydia and Newel, the conflict centered on Lydia's first marriage, which, for all legal and religious purposes, was still in place. So the two courted and hoped for a solution, until one day news reached Lydia of her first husband's death. Finally, the pair could wed. It would be the first wedding performed by Joseph Smith. Later, during the saints' move west, Newel would die at Ponca (what is today Knox County, Nebraska). The loss found Lydia alone and again without means, this time with multiple children, including her son, Jesse, who would eventually pay for her headstone. These are just some of the challenges that Ami sees showing Lydia's strength and independence—qualities Ami both aspires and relates to.

Lydia would find her own means of getting herself and her children across the plains to the church's promised land—Utah. But it would seem that before she made the trek, Newel did have one last bit of aid to offer. He appeared to Lydia in a vision, assuring her that he was in heaven because that's where the prophet needed him, and that she was capable of all the things that lay in front of her. That spiritual confirmation of her faith and her own strength served Lydia well in the years ahead.[81]

Seeking voices from the beyond is a common human desire. Getting a response means that we are not temporal, ephemeral blips; instead, it promises that something of us extends beyond this mortal life. From well before the birth of spiritualism in the 1840s—a movement that popularized things like séances and communing with the dead via mediums—people have reached a hand out into the fog that hangs between this life and whatever comes next. It is in part this same impulse that leads people to visit Lydia's grave to hear her voice or see her appear. It's a fun, light-hearted way to explore the boundaries of reality, of life and death. The fact that, for most people who visit her grave, Lydia is a stranger matters little. Her grave stands out because of its size and the inscription "Not dead but sleeping." Though, according to Ami, the statement probably stands more as a declaration of the LDS belief in the resurrection than a declaration of Lydia's intent to haunt the cemetery.

Every year, thousands of people make trips to spots like Lydia's grave hoping to interact with the other side, but the far more common form of communication with the beyond is what researchers call post-bereavement hallucinations (though I prefer the term post-bereavement communications. There is no need to beg the question and assume an unstable mental state, an assumption that the research itself notes is the primary fear that holds people back from discussing their communications).[82]

Post-bereavement communications can be something as simple as catching a whiff of the scent of a deceased loved one, but they can also be as large as the type of full visual and auditory communication Lydia had with Newel. Several studies suggest that as many as 80 percent of us may experience a post-bereavement communication of some kind in our lives.[83]

While noteworthy, Cyndee Spilker-Jacobson's experience with her friend's recording from Lydia's grave pales in comparison to the more personal communications she has had with the deceased. It is worth mentioning that, unlike her experience with Lydia's grave, these encounters were spontaneous. Consistent with what post-bereavement communication researchers have found, fear of judgment was the primary reason Cyndee kept her own experiences quiet for so long. "Fear of judgment and fear of criticism," she said, "and not being believed or even taking away from the experiences because some of them were so beautiful, and I didn't share them for years because they were very personal." We all fear sharing precious personal experiences, supernatural or not, because there is the chance that other people won't appreciate them, and that lack of appreciation could tarnish them for us. Just think of the last time you tried to share something as simple as a favorite movie with someone, and they didn't pay attention. Maybe they were checking their phone or talking through the film. There is a hard grinding that happens inside of us when the beauty we see in something isn't recognized by others, and it's even worse when others see that beauty as something worthy of mockery. But if there is a place of acceptance we can reach where the opinions of others can't harm our precious experiences, Cyndee eventually found it. Now she shares her experiences freely. Her first communication involved her grandfather when she was a young girl. She was unsure of what was happening, and the experience frightened her. However, the more of these experiences she had, the more she found peace in them. This is also reflected in the research. By and large, these types of otherworldly visitations aren't scary. In fact, they're seen as an important part of the grieving process.[84] This can be seen clearly in Lydia's communication with Newel. The visit seemed to have enabled her to process the heavy trauma of his loss in a positive way.

Speaking to me on the phone late one night, Cyndee told me about visits she received from her deceased husband and a series of visits she had involving her son who died at only a few months old:

> *My son passed when he was four months old. And after he passed away, he came to me. He came to me every night and let me hold him, and he let me feed him, and he said that he would come every night until I was ready to let him go home. And so, after the third night, I felt comfortable....He could go and do what he needed to do, and he didn't come back to me.*

Audibly holding back tears, she added, "So that helped me a ton, because at the time, I just wanted to not exist anymore." It's easy to see why someone would guard an experience like this. While Lydia's community of early LDS pioneers was vocal about visions and other spiritually miraculous events (Newel had once been possessed by a demon that was then exorcised by Joseph Smith), modern society, even in religious communities, tends to balk at such experiences.[85] Rather than simply basking in the beauty of the moment with the person, our own lack of certainty about the nature of the universe often drives us to examine it for evidence. We lose the emotional truth of the moment in our pursuit of the factual truth. But do those two have to be mutually exclusive? Can we cherish the experience and examine it at the same time?

This is exactly what author and immunologist Gerald N. Callahan does in his book *Faith, Madness, and Spontaneous Human Combustion*. Callahan shares his own post-bereavement communication and demonstrates how knowledge, mystery and beauty can coexist:

> *Last Thursday, one of those gray fall days when the starlings gather up and string between the elms around here, my children's mother—dead ten years—walked into a pastry shop where I was buttering a croissant. She ignored me, which she always does, ordered a plain bagel and an almond latte, picked up her food, and, without a glance at me, walked out.*[86]

Callahan said he doesn't see her as often as he did immediately after her suicide, but she still shows up from time to time. He also bluntly states, "I'm not crazy." As he explores his experiences, he argues that immunological memory could be the source of his visitation. Without going into the science of it—though it is fascinating and well worth giving Callahan a read to explore—our immune systems are very detailed self-portraits. Over time, through immunological memory, those closest to us (Newel Knight, Cyndee's son, Gerald's wife) can become a part of that self-portrait. As Callahan says:

> *Among the things we regularly trade with our wives (and the rest of our families for that matter) are viruses—colds, flus, cold sores, to mention only a few....Perhaps that seems trivial—a bit of envelope here, a little DNA there. But over the course of an intimate relationship, we collect a lot of pieces of someone else. And a little of each of those pieces is stored in lymph nodes and in our chromosomes.*
>
> *Until. Until the person we've been communicating with is gone, and we stop gathering bits of someone we love. For a few days or weeks, everything seems pretty much like it was. Then, one day...our defenses slip just a little, and a ghost walks through the door and orders an almond latte.*[87]

Ami Comeford standing at Lydia Knight's grave.

Unlike Lydia's communication with Newel or Cyndee's experience with her son, for Callahan, and for so many people, these experiences are one-sided. They are closer to a snippet of a voicemail than they are to a conversation.

But do these communications have to go both ways? In discussing her connection to Lydia, Ami told me that she often visits Lydia's grave to talk through problems she's having. The St. George cemetery sits just off Utah Technical University campus, so it's just a hop for her to visit her fourth-great-grandmother. "If I'm having a bad day, I go and talk to Lydia," she said. Sitting in her office, I asked Ami, with a bit of hesitation, if she's ever heard Lydia respond during their conversations. She told me:

> *I don't know that she necessarily talks to me. I mean, I certainly haven't had one of those experiences that people say, like, "I saw something." Right? I think it's more a sense of a connection to someone who was in my family line who was probably listening. So I think it's more of me having a sense that there's somebody there listening.*

I've never had a post-bereavement communication, but recently I'd been stuck in one of the biggest moral dilemmas of my life, and I found myself reaching out beyond tangible reality for help. Driving to work, I tried to talk, for the first time in ten years, to someone I couldn't prove was there. I found myself trying to talk to my maternal grandfather. He'd been my best friend growing up, and if there was one person I could pick to talk to from the other side of what we know, he'd be it. Stopping for a red light, I explained the situation to him and told him that I didn't know what to do. I didn't talk for long, just a block or two, but the thing is, it helped. Perhaps, like Ami's experiences with Lydia, it was less about hearing from him and more feeling like maybe he could hear me. But it helped. And I know the logistics don't add up. I know that parts of the conversation were in my head and other parts out loud. I know that I didn't mention the full context of the situation, just broad strokes and vague pleadings, as we often do in prayer and conversations with the dead. I heard no words. I felt no words, not even a chill or presence. But it helped.

Was it simply that the thought of talking to him provided some comfort for my subconscious, calming my mind enough to find the solution to my problem? And even if that's the case, even if it was just my own thought, it was the thought of talking *to him* that helped. It was still my grandfather being alive in my heart and mind (and perhaps my lymph nodes) and just the hope that maybe he could hear me that helped. If that is the case, then isn't it true that the dead do live on, if only in us? If it is only through our memories of them that they can still interact with and impact the world, doesn't that still make them real?

So will visiting the grave of Lydia Knight yield a supernatural experience? I can't say, but I'd be willing to bet that whatever the outcome of someone's visit, it will be more profound and rewarding if they've taken the time to get to know Lydia a bit first, if they've created a little space for her in their heart and mind. Of course, there's no harm in reaching out to someone who already takes up some space in there, even if it's just an exercise in keeping their memory alive.

CHAPTER 7

GRAFTON

Utah's Most Haunted Ghost Town

One of the more surreal moments of my life as a writer and researcher had to be some months back, when I was yelled at by a ninety-year-old woman on Facebook. So you could say this chapter is less the story of Grafton and more the story behind a sweet old woman handing me my ass on social media.

Settled in 1859, Grafton was another pioneer town established as part of the Latter-day Saint cotton mission. As with all western settlements, Grafton's history is more complicated than it might seem at first glance. The town was founded in the shadow of what is now Zion National Park, and the LDS pioneers who established it didn't make things easy on themselves. In addition to regular raids by the Indigenous people whose lands they were encroaching upon, the residents of Grafton had unknowingly chosen to build their homes on a floodplain.[88] So every couple of years, an act of God would just sort of wipe away much of the progress they had made. Still, records from the time—pioneer journals, town notes—indicate that Grafton was largely a happy place where families loved each other, the community supported each other and children ran and played freely in the plentiful summer sun. As historian Ronald S. Morris notes, "They helped each other in times of birth, sickness and death. Money was scarce. Articles of necessity were made by hand or obtained by barter. Harvest time was a community social event. They found enjoyment in work, not in escape from it."[89]

If you visit Grafton today, you can get a sense of what it would have looked like back in the early 1900s. Most of the log homes have been restored.

Grafton church house.

Along with the sandstone church and schoolhouse, these homes have been preserved by the Grafton Heritage Partnership. This is one side of Grafton, the state and church history rich side. The side where settlers are seen as heroes braving a savage land, under attack by a savage people, where faith is the force behind the success that came before the failures and where failures are called hardships—lessons learned at the hand of a loving but firm god. For people like Patti Williams Cauthen and her dear ninety-year-old mother, Dorothy, who grew up in Grafton, this is their Grafton. It is a beautiful place, and despite the tone I started this chapter with, it is real, and it is valid. The way that Dorothy remembers the pioneer settlement she grew up in, "a home of love and joy," is a history worth preserving, an image worth cherishing. And that's just what descendants of Grafton do on a yearly basis. Gathering for a reunion, they eat and share stories that have been passed down to them. As an article in the *Desert News* notes:

> *People alternate coming forward to a lone microphone piped through a single portable speaker. A story is told about a branding implement used to mark cattle in Grafton; a poem is read about a horse with one good eye named Chalkeye that refuses to be broken; a song is sung tongue-in-cheek about the close family relationships of Graftonians (in such a small town, many*

> *of the second generation were related to each other and some families even moved away because of concerns that cousins could begin to marry).*[90]

This Grafton is quaint and wholesome, friendly and bright, but just like people, places don't make flat characters. They are round. Places, perhaps, even more so than people, because they live so much longer lives.

For teenagers from the nearby town of Springdale during the '80s and '90s, Grafton was something entirely different. An abandoned Old West ghost town, Grafton held the promise of escape from the everyday, but it was also more than what those kids wanted it to be. As Adrienne Gates, who grew up in Springdale during the '90s, explained to me:

> *When I was in high school and growing up, we didn't know very much at all about the history of Grafton itself. A lot of kids were related to the people in the cemetery, but we didn't really consider that....It was kind of annoying that it felt haunted and creepy because we wanted to party there....Like, we wanted it to be not that way.*

Unlike most teenage legend tripping outings, where the goal is to encounter something otherworldly, these kids just wanted a place away from the watchful eyes of parents, teachers and church leaders, but the supernatural kept getting in the way. It crept into their weekend bonfires just like they had crept unbidden into the remains of the town.

This is how things started, then: the cycle of folklore inspired legend trips that, in turn, led to memorate, creating new lore, and then new groups of kids legend tripping kicked in, and suddenly kids were holding séances in the schoolhouse and playing with Ouija boards inside of the "house of evil" where dear old Dorothy grew up. But again, the catch is, despite my tone, the Grafton of spooky sounds and creepy feelings, dark nights and cold chills, is real. It was a place filled with coming of age and self-discovery, and it, too, is a valid history worth preserving. It's easy to simplify people and places. The world we inhabit is vast and, now more than perhaps at any moment in history, both complex and complicated. Our minds have to try to map things out to keep us safe and to keep us sane. We need to label things, mark the dangerous terrain and the safe harbors out on the maps of our minds. This is why it is not only an act of courage to let someone else show us who they are—and for us to actually accept and believe them—but an act of extraordinary trust. When we do this, we are handing control of our map over to someone else. We are letting them define part of our reality. When

Right: View of Zion National Park from the interior of a Grafton pioneer home.

Below: The makings of a bonfire in Grafton.

The "House of Evil" in Grafton.

someone tells us they aren't who we've painted them to be, it's easier—and it feels safer—to turn from the feeling of cognitive dissonance created by the conflict in our minds and retreat to the safety of how we already see things. The same goes for places. I imagine that, for Dorothy, it is easier to see the ghost town of Grafton as a lie created by people ignorant of the wonderful history she remembers. For some of those Springdale teenagers, the stories teachers and church leaders told them of noble pioneer Grafton were, perhaps, a bit boring and irrelevant when compared to the cold chill creeping up their spine or the prospect of a wild night out where they could really let loose and do some self-exploration.

All too often, however, both of these ideas of Grafton are forgetting an important third side to the picture. Long before the first white person set eyes on what is now called Zion National Park or foot in Grafton, the area was inhabited by various Indigenous groups. According to the National Park Service, "Human use of the Zion National Park landscape dates back to at least 6,000 B.C.E. Archeologists have divided this long span of human history into four cultural periods, each characterized by distinctive technological and social adaptations."[91] First came the Virgin Branch of Ancestral Puebloan and Parowan Fremont groups. The archaeological record shows that these groups slowly shifted from nomadic to more agricultural in

The basement of the "House of Evil" in Grafton.

nature. Eventually they were driven out by weather or competition. As the National Park Service notes:

> *Extended droughts in the 11th and 12th centuries, interspersed with catastrophic flooding, may have made horticulture impossible in this arid region. Some researchers have suggested that* [the Ancestral Puebloan and Fremont] *could not successfully compete for wild resources with the more mobile Numic language speakers (such as the Southern Paiute and Ute) who were in the region by at least C.E. 1100.*[92]

As for the Southern Paiute and Ute tribes who inhabited the region after that time, records show that they primarily lived around the canyon, not in it.

It is difficult to pin down Indigenous lore and history. Digging through academic databases, Google deep dives, interviews with Indigenous people of various tribes—all highlight, intentionally or unintentionally, the same problem. It is the problem of a contemporary people who have been marginalized and misrepresented to the point of vanishing and then treated as if they had indeed vanished, treated as if they weren't actively fighting to retain and regain their cultural identity, beliefs and a fraction of their rights. As Joseph Whitson, the creator of Indigenous Geotags, a website dedicated to addressing the ways the outdoor retail industry affects Indigenous culture and history, notes, these are a people who were put through systematic cultural erasure:

> *Mukuntuweap, known as Zion Canyon, is the homeland and a sacred place to the Southern Paiute. Zion National Park, more than most parks I have looked at, placed the Paiute firmly in the past—even labeling the section* [of their website] *on Native people "People of the Past."…U.S. policy may have forced the Paiute onto reservations, and the National Park designation may have…attempted to erase the indigenous history, but none of this changes the fact that this is illegally taken Paiute land.*[93]

Whitson acknowledges the complexity of the issue, noting that the parks system and the outdoor recreation industry perform good environmental advocacy; however, he, and many others, feel that good doesn't make up for the damage being done to the culture and lives of contemporary Indigenous people.

One of the most interesting elements of this complexity is the "vibe" people get in both Zion and Grafton. If you were to look at the overwhelming majority of online content with social media tags related to Zion National Park, you would find an abundance of statements like "beautiful," "calm," "awe-inspiring," "rejuvenating," "breathtaking," even "spiritually awakening." And I agree the land is beautiful. The canyon and the formations in it are breathtaking. I've spent a lot of time in Zion National Park and in Springdale. To me, the canyon has the same feeling I got growing up next to American Fork Canyon: a quiet sense of adventure. The town of Springdale itself feels quaint and artistic. But that is what these places feel like to me. Not necessarily to the locals. Or to you.

If you ask the Springdale teenagers from the '80s and '90s, Grafton was eerie. Some parts of it felt evil. Many of those I talked to simply said there was a darkness there or that it made their hair stand up on end. If you ask Adrienne Gates, local teens weren't the only ones to experience those vibes in Grafton or nearby Zion. "There's a lot of energy in Zion. I hear a lot of people talk about it. They think it's maybe the opposite end of the vortex. That it is Sedona's sister." In fact, the internet is awash with information about the spiritually healing effects of Sedona, Arizona. As VisitSedona.com says, "The majestic red rock scenery and evergreen vegetation are two reasons for the unique energy of Sedona and its tangible regenerative and inspirational effects." If some people believe Zion National Park is the

Pioneer home in Grafton.

View of pioneer home in Grafton from the interior of another pioneer home.

opposite end of that vortex, that would indicate that they believe Zion is a very dark and dangerous place.

Adrienne, who was partially raised in an Indigenous home on her father's side, furthered this idea while telling me about her time working the front desk of a Springdale hotel:

> *A lot of people, when they come to Zion, they come for a spiritual experience, and they're trying to have all of these Instagram photos and their bucket list hikes, but they don't really understand that the Indigenous people did not go into the canyon really at all. If they did, it was rare, and it was definitely only during the daytime. So the place itself is actually really hardcore as far as the energy of the canyon, and when I talked to people who come* [to Zion] *being like "Oh, Sedona and crystal power," they'll be like, "whoa! Zion is super heavy and dark and dense, and I didn't think it was going to be like this, but it's kind of scary here." Or, "At night I didn't feel the same way that I did in Sedona, it wasn't enlightening." I'm like, yeah, people didn't go into the canyon when it was just Indigenous people. I think that there is some of that when you get to Grafton.... When I was working as a clerk in a store or in the hotel, just giving people advice on where to go* [while visiting Zion], *and they'd say, "Oh, I did go to Grafton, and that was really crazy. We went at night." And they'd tell us some little story, and we'd laugh like I told you.... We never had anyone come back and say, "I spent the night there," or "It was awesome" and "it felt enlightening" or "uplifting." Everyone was always kind of "Argh!"*

She went on to talk about how, even though she grew up in Springdale, when she comes back to visit, she stays with friends in nearby Rockville:

> *The difference between being in Springdale and Rockville is really different, like the sunlight going behind the canyon walls, there's just something that changes. I was really always climbing out of my skin to get out of Springdale. I left as soon as I was eighteen. I just didn't feel like I should be there. But when I go to Rockville, it's a totally different feeling. It's welcoming, the light stays all evening because there's no cliffs, and you get this kind of different vibe. And then as soon as I drive out from Rockville to Grafton, I feel the energy shift* [back].

Hearing Adrienne's mimicking of tourists' "Sedona and crystal power," I can't help but think of the new agers who appropriate Native culture and how much this misunderstanding of Zion feels similar to their misuse of sage and sweat lodges and their refusal to seek out cultural information from actual Indigenous individuals. I discuss this more in the chapter on Route 666 and the chapter on skinwalkers.

One particular Indigenous person I spoke with about Zion and Grafton was native archaeology teacher Kaye Feather Robinson. When I asked her about the darkness I'd heard people say the Paiute and those who came before them felt in regards to the area, she said, "Well, the Indigenous people thought that it wasn't a good place to live. And it was haunted." She related the Paiute story of the brave who went into the canyon because his people were starving and he wanted to find deer or other food in the canyon, but the bear god didn't like this and chased the brave. Sinawava, the wolf god, saved the young brave by raising up the great white throne (one of Zion's most notable attractions), and the bear god slid down, leaving his bloody claw marks on the throne. Feather added that "when you walk down there, you can still hear the wolf god and the bear god chasing each other, and that's where rocks come down in." She also mentioned that "Anasazi valley…has been nothing but conflict. So a darkness will stay there simply because, I mean, from my Native belief, simply because those spirits were never sung home. And the belief that when you die, you don't recognize that you're dying. So your spirit hangs around." From Feather's perspective, even as someone from a different tribe (she's Blackfeet, not Paiute), the reasons behind Zion and Grafton's darkness are spiritual ones, rooted in oral history and belief.

The state- and church-history-rich side of Grafton has its own dark spots. One of the darkest deals with the death of two young girls, Loretta and Elizabeth. One fine summer day in 1866, the two girls and a younger girl, Sara, were playing on a makeshift swing hanging from a large tree branch. At first, Sara rode on Elizabeth's lap. Eventually, Sara ran home, while Loretta and Elizabeth kept swinging. Before Sara had made it all the way home, however, the branch gave way, falling to the ground and killing both Loretta and Elizabeth. A song produced by the Western Folklife Center recreates the story, emphasizing that just as the girls went back and forth on the swing, now they must go back and forth between this life and the next. One tale, told by former Grafton resident Vilo Demille and incorporated into the song, goes into great detail about her specific encounter with the girls.

One night, in 1927 while playing an old childrens' game, Run Sheepy Run, Vilo closed her eyes for the other kids to hide, and when she opened them, she saw two girls she didn't recognize. She recalls they were both

Left: Kaye Feather Robinson speaking at a political rally in St. George, 2017.

Below: The tombstone of Loretta and Elizabeth in Grafton cemetery.

Opposite: Reflection of the Grafton church house in the window of a pioneer home.

in long, white dresses with long, white hair. She went to chase them, and they disappeared near a fence. "One went through the poles that made the fence," Vilo noted, "and the other went right over the top." Reflecting on the story, Vilo, who was twelve years old at the time, said, "These two girls that are buried here in [Grafton] cemetery, I thought quite a few times, I wondered if it was the two girls that I saw."[94]

Stories like the girls on the swing and those told by the Springdale teens drew people to the ghost town. As Adrienne mentioned to me, over time, her and her friends started to see teens from St. George coming to Grafton, not to party but to experience the spooky happenings that had ruined the Springdale teens' parties. Of course, the introduction of the internet changed the spreading of urban legends for Grafton, just like it did for urban legends and folklore everywhere else. As folklorist Lynne McNiell says, "All of our rumors and legends…[are] now being shared in a venue where just the act of sharing it turns it into documented cultural data."[95] Now you can do an internet search for "Utah ghost towns" or "haunted places in Utah" and find an avalanche of lists like "Five Haunted Places in Utah" or "Six Spooky Utah Locations" or "The Most Haunted Places in Utah." Some of these articles come from places you'd expect—local news sites, for example—but others are found in places stretching from a home security website[96] to an RV lifestyle website[97] to a site that seems to exist just to sell

Wooden tombstones in Grafton cemetery.

Utah-themed T-shirts.[98] There are, of course, plenty of websites dedicated solely to the sharing of all things supernatural. One of my favorite stories (though I haven't been able to find its original source) mentioned a mountain biker who tried to spend the night in Grafton, unaware of its supernatural lore, and was driven out by ghosts. Still other stories tell of phantom gunshots (thought to be echoes from battles between settlers and Indigenous tribes). Many online stories (and many stories people told me, for that matter) deal with the sound of ghostly children laughing or crying.

The cemetery at Grafton, located a little more than three hundred yards before the town proper, is its own creature. For many locals, it's just like any other cemetery. It is a peaceful place where they can go to visit their loved ones. For those without a connection to the interred, it's a picture-perfect haunted space with old wooden and sandstone grave markers planted in hard red dirt and surrounded by a rickety old wood fence. And yet, for others like Feather, it is a darker place. The first time Feather and her son, who she described as her Spock—very logical—went to the cemetery at Grafton, they were both overwhelmed by the feeling:

> *So the first time we went out to Grafton, we went to that cemetery they've got there. My son walked around for a minute, and he said, "Mom, we*

Left: Stone tombstone in Grafton cemetery.

Right: Wooden tombstone in Grafton cemetery.

got to get the hell out of here. This place is really bad."...And he goes, "Nope, Mom, we gotta get out of here." And he loves ghost towns, loves ghost towns, but we couldn't get out of that cemetery fast enough. Because of the darkness. And, you know, you've got a couple of Natives that were buried there that were killed at Pipe Spring....One of the things white people did, you know, because all Indians look alike and sound alike and whatever, but if an Indian murdered somebody, they don't go after the person that murdered, they'd kill the whole tribe. And it could be the wrong tribe! They don't care. "We're just going to kill Indians." And so there's a story up in Pipe Springs that some Navajos and even some of those [white] *people that were killed at Pipe Springs were buried* [in Grafton]. *And the one lady that I see when I go there, I see the woman there, and she was the woman that was pregnant and was killed,* [a] *white woman. She was tied to a wagon wheel, and she was killed and this was Navajos, but they claimed that to retaliate they went out and they killed, they're not really sure if they were Paiute or Navajo that they killed or buried there. I mean, "They all look alike, they're all Indians."*

> *And so that cemetery has a real darkness about it. It's one of the very few places I would never be there at night. I would never…*

Different groups having conflicting feelings about a location isn't new. Almost anytime there is a war, one group leaves with a much darker feeling toward the location than the other, and that feeling gets passed down in their folk traditions and lore. The same thing can happen with the passage of time. Sometimes this is due to an erosion of knowledge. We forget the history, the stories of a place, and something of that place is lost for the next generation. That generation then goes on to make it their own, with their own history and stories.

When I posted photos from a trip to Grafton on social media, I was only thinking about those teenagers in '90s Grafton. So I labeled one particular house what they had called it: "the house of evil." Thankfully, Dorothy Williams, at ninety years old, was there (exclamation points at the ready) to teach me about the loving home she grew up in, the same one in the picture, a home she'd *never* heard called a house of evil. And just in case I didn't hear her, several of Dorothy's relatives were there to back her up. They were going to make sure Dorothy's Grafton was not forgotten.

Still other voices, some silenced long ago, some alive and screaming but muffled by political and cultural forces, are not as easily heard. Sometimes, it takes the rediscovery of a forgotten history or a shifting of the lens through which we look at a history to change a place for the incoming generation.

As society works at coming to terms with the crimes early Americans committed against the Indigenous peoples of this land, we will come to look at some places, like Mount Rushmore, or Route 666, or Zion National Park in radically different ways from past generations. It would seem that the key isn't to reject any of these versions of a place. Rather, we should look at them like shards of light coming off a prism, each illuminating a different facet of a place—some highlighting factual truths, others cultural or personal truths. It is when we outright reject a version altogether that we lose something of the whole of a place, along with the opportunity to learn something profound about ourselves.

CHAPTER 8

THE SECRETS OF THE MOUNTAIN MEADOWS MASSACRE

Vengeance is mine; I will repay, saith the Lord.
Romans 12:19

It feels inappropriate to picture the members of the Baker-Fancher party, their hopes and plans for the future packed into covered wagons, dug in, firing at and taking fire from the Mormon settlers of Southern Utah. Those same wagons, circled in defense, provided little but vital protection from the Mormons who had fallen upon the wagon train. The siege lasted days. Thirsty, tired and terrified, the Baker-Fancher party would have felt relief at the sight of a white flag of truce. They allowed members of the mob to enter their defenses to bring them food and water. In addition, the Mormons told them they'd allow the party to leave in peace if they handed over their weapons and allowed the Mormons to escort them out of the area. Was there hesitance? Were rifles handed over by shaking hands? Did the members of the Baker-Fancher party trust the Mormons' word, or did they just see no other way out? How much did each step away from their defensive position weigh in their mind? After the Mormons had escorted the party some distance, they turned and fired on the now-defenseless group.

Dawn sat just over the hills as I stepped out of my car and headed down the paved path that leads from the parking area to the official monument honoring the victims of the Mountain Meadows Massacre. Frost spotted the hard ground and brush. Small patches of snow sat unmelted by the

Above: The current Mountain Meadows Massacre Monument.

Opposite: Close up of the cairn at the Mountain Meadows Massacre Monument.

approaching spring. Standing in front of the monument, I shifted one hand from my camera to my pocket, then back again, trying to keep them warm.

The main monument, a cairn—a cemented pile of stones—surrounded by a series of small gravestones, marks the south corner of the meadow. A dirt path stretches around the area where many of the at least 120 members of the Baker-Fancher migrant wagon train were slaughtered by the Nauvoo Legion (the Utah Territorial Militia) under the command of John D. Lee and Isaac C. Haight in the fall of 1857. Reasons for the massacre vary depending on who you ask, and early disinformation (along with destruction of records) by the LDS church have made figuring things out a muddled affair. Most theories fall into a handful of camps: the Mormon settlers, who would have still vividly recalled Governor Boggs's "extermination order," were scared of attack; the Mormons, jealous of the wealth of the Baker-Fancher party, sought to rob them; or years of inflammatory rhetoric and xenophobic stances turned normal men into a bloodthirsty mob.

A series of plaques and markers spot a path around the meadow, providing details about the victims and the attacks. The day of my visit, a loose band of cows wandered the area, munching on frost-crusted grass. I don't know what I expected to feel. People had told me that the massacre site felt everything

from peaceful to sad and even dark, but honestly, I didn't feel any of that. Local resident Les Sperry noted, "I've been there several times and have never experienced anything too supernatural. But there is a deep stillness and sadness there. It's heavy and burdensome." Another local, Pat Buck, added, "I have been there twice. The spirits are very close; you don't see them, but you feel them. It's a sad place, and I really felt like crying. I doubt I will ever go back, but I respect what I felt there." I had come to Mountain Meadows with the mindset that I should feel something. I paused partway through the end of my first walk around the loop to focus on the emotion of the area, but the land itself felt like any other cow pasture. It was physically cold, but that was it.

Many people claim to have experienced more than an emotional feeling at the massacre site. M. Rick Erickson's grandmother told him stories about voices and lights at the site:

> *Our grandmother spent a lot of her childhood on farms the Leavitt and Burgess families owned at the Meadows (1919–1920s). She told us stories of walking between the different homesteads in the evenings, having to cross parts of the massacre sites, and would see small blue and white lights moving among the sagebrush as if with a purpose and in seemingly erratic patterns. She also told of* [her] *and her sisters hearing sounds of women weeping that would come from different parts of the area at dusk or dark. Our grandmother was a very intelligent woman, valedictorian of her class at Dixie College, and not given to hyperbole or exaggeration. She would tell us these stories matter-of-factly.*

Stories of ghostly apparitions or sounds at the site date back to as early as just after the massacre. One of the earliest narratives involves one of the families who kept a child from the Baker-Fancher group who hadn't been slaughtered (the Nauvoo Legion spared seventeen children whom they felt were too young to be able to remember or tell of what had happened. There was an eighteenth child, but at the last minute, militia members decided she was too old and shot her as she stood next to the rest of the children).[99] The children who lived were taken by LDS families for two years before the U.S. Army freed them and returned them to their relatives in Arkansas. One of these LDS families was the Peter B. Fife household. Mrs. Leon Fonnesbeck related the following story to Austin E. Fife in 1939, and he later published it (as part of a collection of Mormon folklore) in *California Folklore Quarterly*:

Peter B. Fife lived at Fort Cove. He took into his home one of the seventeen children who had been saved from the massacre. One day the child was sleeping, and a woman dressed in white from head to foot appeared to Mrs. Fife, who was just outside the house. The woman asked if she could see "my baby." Mrs. Fife told her that the child was sleeping and that she might go in to see it. The woman entered the house. Shortly after, Mrs. Fife also went in the house, but the woman was not there.[100]

A casual interpretation of this narrative would seem to indicate that the spectral woman, having seen that her child was safe, went on to rest in peace, as she is not recorded to have appeared again. However, the reality of the seventeen children's treatment in the LDS homes should cast some doubt on that. As Captain James Lynch's official affidavit from 1859 stated, when the army reclaimed the children, they were "in a most wretched condition, half starved, half naked, filthy, infested with vermin, and their eyes diseased from the cruel neglect to which [they] had been exposed."[101] In this light, the story of the mother visiting her child becomes more about a community, perhaps, trying to make itself feel better about this great evil that had become a part of its history. Note that the vanishing woman in the tale is not depicted as angry, evil or spooky; rather, she is dressed in all white and behaves quite politely. We've all done things that hurt people, and there is a sense of relief that comes if we can later see that the person we harmed is okay, even more so if they don't seem to hold any animosity toward us. Here we have a piece of lore that could provide a sense of relief, even of absolution, for the LDS settlers about what they'd done to the Baker-Fancher party.

Many of these stories have fallen from the community consciousness as Southern Utah has grown and as the LDS church has attempted to acknowledge the massacre at Mountain Meadows. While some people have expressed skepticism at the LDS church's motives behind building the monument (specifically that they built it primarily as a means to control the narrative), for many people in the community, the building and dedication of the monument served to alleviate any guilt they may have felt for the crimes of their ancestors. As local resident Marilyn Burgess Fenn said, "There are no ghost stories....The meadows were dedicated when the monument went up....The Fancher party descendants along with the Lee family [have] worked hard to heal the lives and hearts of their ancestors." Yet the stories still persist.

Regardless of the loss of individual narratives, the idea of the land at Mountain Meadows being haunted is still very much alive. In fact, the

Mountain Meadows.

general idea as noted by Birney Hoffman in *Zealots of Zion* in 1931 still holds true: "There are stories of unseen wagons that creak slowly along the arroyo where once was an emigrant road, of the roll of ghostly gunfire echoing from the rocky hills, of moonless nights made hideous by the screams of woman and children." Many of the stories I gathered match with these ideas of phantom sounds—gunfire and woman screams in particular. The stories of these screams aren't limited to LDS pioneers and descendants. In his book, *Southern Paiute: A Portrait*, W.L. Hebner shares the story of a young Paiute woman named Eleanor Tom:

> *As a child, Eleanor Tom, a Paiute Indian born in 1924, regularly walked through the meadows with a friend. She recalled: "We weren't scared. But my grandmother told us if you have to go through there, you better hurry and get through before it gets dark. Because she said you could hear crying and screaming at night."*[102]

The internet has only aided in keeping this general atmosphere of Mountain Meadows present in people's minds. As an article from OnlyinYourState.com notes, "Mostly, people report an eerie feeling of being watched. But, some say that they hear the cries of children, women screaming, and men shouting." The article goes on to mention people "seeing a woman walking across the meadow, acting as though she's searching for something....There are a few accounts of an older man, seen in broad daylight at the memorial, sobbing. He's...thought to be the ghost of John D. Lee." Of course, as with most such articles, there is no citation or reference given for the origin of these tales.

In addition to clickbait articles like the one on Only in Your State, comments and message boards have proven an excellent web tool for keeping lore alive and even finding original memorate. Sadly, use of screen names in such places makes tracking down the commenters strenuous at best. Still, if we take the people behind the screen names at their word (which one still has to do when told memorate face to face), these comments can provide a new vein to the lore.

One commenter simply identified as Somedude noted, "The area is haunted. Lights moving among the fields and sagebrush at night. Sounds of women and children weeping can be heard. A palpable sense of fear and foreboding as well. Not at the monument site, but the locations of the killings further to the north." This provides another voice echoing the lore of women and children weeping, as well as the additional information about locations "further to the north." Another commenter, Christine, shared an experience she had in 2016: "[I] visited last week and heard a whisper as I walked the circumference of the field to the family monument. Ever since leaving in the quiet of mornings or as I fall asleep I hear distant screams, crying and gunshots." Even more recently, in July 2020, J Blackby noted, "I went there in broad daylight and as we were walking around we kept hearing and seeing rocks being kicked as [if] someone unseen shuffled behind us in the pathway... We were the only two people there... Gave me chills." Blackby's experience is reminiscent of an older piece of Mountain Meadows lore from Hoffman, involving people seeing footprints left in the snow by ghosts.[103]

A number of mediums or "intuitives" have investigated Mountain Meadows and cited everything from feeling the pain of victims to experiencing full visions of the massacre and its aftermath. It isn't only the "spiritually sensitive" who see or hear things; rather, it is often people with some connection to the land. Local resident Casey Adams never noticed anything strange himself but mentioned that "a very good friend...who is a direct descendant of some of the people from the massacre, has very, very bad vibes and has seen things in Holt's Canyon in conjunction with the massacre." It makes sense that having a connection to a haunted location

Mountain Meadows.

would increase the likelihood of someone experiencing something. Whether you look at it from the spiritual standpoint that a connection to the place or event increases a person's sensitivity to the energies there or from a more academic perspective that someone with a connection is more prone to enter the area in a preconditioned mindset—a mindset that makes such experiences more likely—an individual connection to the place does seem significant. This is magnified with a place like Mountain Meadows, a place of violence and guilt.

Among the many types of supernatural lore associated with the massacre is that of a curse that fell upon the LDS settlers who participated in it. My good friend, and wonderful writer, Marianne Hales Harding is a descendant of one of the perpetrators of the massacre. Talking about Mountain Meadows, she mentioned something her grandfather had said: "My grandfather always used to tell my mom not to worry because she was the fifth generation since the massacre, and the sins would be on the head of four generations from the massacre participants." The idea of a curse lasting for four generations is found in the Old Testament. The idea of a curse on the members of the Nauvoo Legion who murdered the Baker-Fancher party seems to be centered on the town of New Harmony. In fact, it was via a former resident of New Harmony that I first heard of the curse.

Located twenty-eight miles, by modern roads, from the Mountain Meadows monument, New Harmony is a small town of only 212 people as of 2019. There are a handful of other towns equally close to the massacre site, and militia members came from across southwestern Utah, so why should lore of the curse have developed to focus primarily on New Harmony? The answer, perhaps, can be found in one particular account of the beginning of the events at Mountain Meadows.

Militia leaders had planned to use the local Natives as scapegoats for the first attack on the Baker-Fancher party. Whether the Nauvoo Legion was able to persuade any Paiutes to join them in the attack is up for debate, but the fact that legion members dressed themselves up to look like Natives is not.[104] In fact, it was fear that some of the survivors of the first attack had discerned the true identities of the attackers that led to the order to kill the remaining members of the party.[105] However, members of the Baker-Fancher party weren't the only individuals to spot the attackers' true identity. In *A History of Utah's American Indians*, Gary Tom and Ronald Holt printed excerpts from several Paiute oral histories. One such history came from a 1998 interview with Paiute Clifford Jake, who recalled a story told to him by Paiute Isaac Hunkup. The story goes that two brothers were hunting deer in Pine Valley when they heard gunshots. Exploring what they'd heard, they found "a wagon train and the people were shooting and killing the wagon train people."[106] The two brothers then witnessed the attackers rob their victims. Following the murderers at a distance, "they followed them till they get to the place to where they are going to change their clothes…to New Harmony.…They took off their Indian outfits…and they were white people.…They were white people that done it." This narrative disputes the earliest of Mormon apologetics about the massacre, namely that the initial attack had been perpetrated by the Paiute. In fact, this is a point Hunkup's story details, noting that the brothers returned to the tribe to warn them: "We are going to get blamed, going to get blamed for what those white people did. There were no Indians in that massacre."[107] This story also identifies New Harmony as the return location of the murderers from the first attack, and that could at least provide some explanation for the curse lore being primarily centered on the residents of New Harmony. Local Native Kaye Feather Robinson (though she is Blackfeet, not Piaute) explained that, according to some Native beliefs, the militiamen who returned to New Harmony will be stuck reincarnating into New Harmony until they realize and accept the errors of what they did.

New Harmony isn't the only cursed location, however. The very soil at Mountain Meadows itself is said to be cursed. As Juanita Brooks notes in *The Mountain Meadows Massacre* (my favorite treatise on the subject):

> *A general belief was that because of the blood that had been shed there, God had cursed the land, so that nothing could grow. What had been a meadow of deep, luxuriant grass, became desolate, a dry, gravelly waste, barren of any vegetation. Students of soil erosion point to this as a classic example. Here, they say, the land was overgrazed, the protective covering removed so that...all the precious top soil drained. But old-timers knew better. They understood the deeper, more fundamental reasons which were tied up with man's evil deeds and God's stamp of disapproval.*[108]

This idea of guilt and "God's stamp of disapproval" in a highly religious area could be the most telling element of the lore.

The guilt from and denial of the Mountain Meadows Massacre have haunted not only Southern Utah but also the LDS church since the event happened. They have been cited as the reason behind the demolition of the first and second memorials built to honor the victims, both built by U.S. Army units, not local residents. The first memorial, a cairn twelve feet high, was constructed after Major James H. Carleton and his cavalry unit finished burying the remains of thirty-four of the massacre victims, which had been left out or buried in shallow graves and then dug up and strewn about by wolves and other animals. On top of the cairn, the soldiers had placed a wooden cross inscribed with a scripture from the book of Romans: "Vengeance is mine; I will repay, saith the Lord." As Casey W. Olsen notes in *The Evolution of History: Changing Narratives of the Mountain Meadows Massacre*, "Local Mormons likely viewed the monument with disdain. It stood as a towering public memorial of a crime which most of them wished had never occurred, and which some of them had sworn to keep a secret."[109] Reporting on the destruction of the monument, the

People place small personal memorials, like this cross and scripture, at the monument.

Salt Lake Tribune noted, "The monument was destroyed by the Mormons, who could not stand such a rebuke of their diabolical guilt."[110] The *Tribune* wasn't the only source to call out the guilt of the Mormons. There are a number of folk songs from the time that seem to scald the church and the state. Brooks cites one such song:

Come all good men of freedom, and to my song give ear
And of the dreadful massacre you presently shall hear…

In Indian garb and colors those bloody hounds were seen
To attack the little train all on the meadows green
They were attacked in the morning, and as they got under way
Forthwith corralled their wagons and fought in blood all day.

When Lee, the leader of the band, his words to them did give
That if their arms they would give up, he'd surely let them live
And as their arms they did give up and started for Cedar City
He rushed on them in Indian style, Oh what a human pity!

They melted down with one accord like wax before the flame
Men and women, old and young, O Utah, blush for shame!
To see mothers and their children lie bleeding in their gore
Oh, such an awful sight I think was never seen before.

This life will soon be over and another coming on
And the perpetrators of the deed must suffer for the wrong
'Tis true they do deny it, and the crime they will disclaim
To get out of it the best they can, the Indians bear the blame.[111]

Up until the LDS church built the current memorial in 1999, it seems that the church and the majority of the community worked with dedication to cover up, or at least avoid, the history associated with Mountain Meadows. As Brooks, a devout Mormon herself, noted in 1950:

A number of reputable Mormon Scholars have begun research on the subject, only to be turned away from it for one reason or another. Two of these men have said that they discontinued because they were "counseled" with such vigor to leave it alone that they felt sure that to continue would cost them not only their positions in the church schools, but their membership in the church itself.[112]

She went on to point out, "It seems that, once having taken a stand and put forth a story, the leaders of the Mormon church have felt that they should maintain it, regardless of all the evidence to the contrary."[113] The idea here would seem to be that time heals all wounds—that if the massacre isn't discussed or investigated, then people might just forget it, and it will go away. However, while some wounds might heal with time, others, worse wounds, vicious in nature and infected with neglect, only grow more grotesque. It isn't until the wounds are reopened, cleaned and properly taken care of that these injuries can at last heal.

Ghosts feel this, too, at least according to common folklore. As folklorist Jeannie Banks Thomas notes, "A ghost returning to complete unfinished business is a common and widespread motif."[114] Popular movies like *The Grudge*, the Patrick Swayze/Demi Moore classic *Ghost* and the Ricky Gervais comedy *Ghost Town* focus their stories on the dead who cannot rest until their business is complete. Television shows like *Ghost Whisperer* and *Medium* share the same formula. In addition to the motherly ghost who appeared to Mrs. Fife, wanting to check on her baby, other stories show this unfinished business motif is present in the Mountain Meadows lore. One example from Brooks mentions a "woman's specter [who] moved among the scrub brush night after night, as though forever searching for something—her baby, perhaps, or a missing, unburied bone that had been dragged away by wolves."[115] This story can highlight the guilt the community felt about the taking of the children and the lack of burial provided for the murdered.

Looking into both the facts and the stories from events like the Mountain Meadows Massacre does more than just aid in healing wounds. Reopening them can help us learn from the mistakes of the past. Wounds, dark moments, tragedy: literature and art focus on these moments and ideas so much not because writers and artists are all depressed sadists but because these tragedies are the best terrain to explore the broken parts of humanity, the parts of us that make us capable of horrors and atrocities.

In her conclusion to *The Mountain Meadows Massacre*, Brooks says:

> *Perhaps when all is finally known, the Mountain Meadows Massacre will be a classic study in mob psychology or the effects of war hysteria. It seems to be a clear case of how a group, stirred and angered by reports only half true, frenzied by mistaken zeal to protect their homes and families and to defend their church, were led to do what none singly would have done under normal conditions.*

Stone marker at Mountain Meadows Massacre Monument.

Mob mentality, war hysteria, mistaken zeal: these are within each of us. Somewhere in a corner of you and me, we have the capability to do that which we never would have thought possible. It is close to there that we can also find our desire to hide our mistakes, to be offended when others shine a light on them. When we look at the supernatural lore surrounding the Mountain Meadows Massacre, we see both our desire to be forgiven by those we have harmed and our struggle to acknowledge the truths and face the work that must be done if we are to be forgiven. We see, in a community and religion centered on the family, subconscious acknowledgment of the pain felt by the families of the Baker-Fancher party, the cries of mothers who would never get to see their children grow up, the panicked footsteps in the snow of husbands searching for their wives.

When I arrived at the Mountain Meadows monument, I noted that I didn't feel anything but the temperature. But as I left, as I passed a memorial plaque designating the resting place of a child's skull, I found myself feeling a weighty sadness for those families torn apart by the massacre and a deep gratitude for the fact that I am still able to go home to my own. Pulling out of the parking lot, I stopped for a moment, reached for my phone, and sent two quick text messages: one to my son's mother, asking her to give him an extra-long hug and tell him his daddy loves him; another to my wife, thanking her for being the person she is.

CHAPTER 9

THE WATSON HOUSE

They'd gone into the cellar of the Watson house to check for termites, a logical precaution when purchasing an older home. Rick Atkin's partner at the time, Daniel, who was six foot six, decided to stay outside rather than duck to fit in the small room. So just Rick and the general contractor stooped down in. As they looked at the inner workings of the 110-year-old home, they heard something above them. Old homes are bound to make noise, but this was clear and sounded like someone walking from one side of the room above them to the other.

> *We heard creaking…from that room in that far corner and* [it] *walk*[ed] *to the front door. We all stopped, and we're like,* What the heck is that? *The general contractor turned to me, and he's like, "Is there somebody in the house," and I said, "Daniel probably went inside."*

Then Rick joked, "Maybe it's haunted." When they resurfaced, he asked Daniel if he'd gone inside for something. Not only had Daniel not gone inside, but every door to the home was locked. No one could have been inside.

This was the first of a handful of experiences Rick had with the home's previous owner, the deceased Dan Watson. The home itself was built in 1908 and has been in the Watson family for generations. Dan's father, Daniel Clark Watson Sr., known by most as Clark, ran the local pharmacy and served as mayor of St. George for three terms. As Rick noted, the senior Watson was "very eccentric, wore gold…drove a gold car." With its large yard and

The Watson house in St. George.

notable community members, the Watson house served as a sort of unofficial community center. Of course, the Atkins themselves have a long history in St. George. In fact, both families had known each other well through the generations. As Rick told me, "Our family has been here forever....[They] came down here like 170 years ago. And so they knew the Watsons."

Rick grew up in St. George but attended school out of state at Harvard University before living and working in Salt Lake. Though life had taken him away from St. George, it was the Watson house that brought him back.

> *Dan Watson* [was an] *amazing member of the community, heavily involved in the university. He never married. When he passed away, he wanted to sell the house to create a scholarship for students at the university.* [But] *nobody in the* [Watson] *family wanted to buy it....Other people wanted to buy it, knock it down, and build duplexes here. And I was just like, "I can't let that happen."*

Dan's connection to the university is well documented. He served as the assistant to Dixie College president Ferron C. Losee starting in 1970, a position he'd hold for the next four college presidents. His scholarship, the Daniel Clark Watson Scholarship, is awarded to one male music major each year. Sitting in the living room of the Watson house chatting with me, Rick emphasized what a generous and kind person Dan had been:

> *He always rented this house out, or he would stay here and then he'd rent out rooms to college students. My uncle, my mom's brother (I didn't know this till after) had rented a room. And Dan...gave him some money to help him move to his first job. He was a prolific writer, the most beautiful handwriting...He was always sending letters to people, and people were sending letters back....That front yard was the community park, essentially. Every person I know used to play here. It was such a big lawn....So this house was open; it was for everybody. And what I understand about his dad, I think his dad was very much the same way.*

When I asked Rick what he knew about Dan never marrying, he told me something he'd heard from a local friend. He said, "What I heard, because one of my friends grew up across the street, and he said to her that he found love once [with] a woman in college, but she didn't love him back. And he could never marry after that." The idea of a man so heartbroken when he found himself, as Annie Dillard would say, "holding one half of a love" that he never recovered could lead us to picture a lonely hermit walled off from the world that had hurt him, but marriage is only one metric for measuring the fullness of a life—and a faulty one at that (how many people have wasted away, trapped by societal standards, in a miserable marriage?). Rather, Dan Watson's life overflowed with family, friends and community. As his obituary notes:

> *Dan Watson was dearly loved by his siblings, nieces and nephews and grandnieces and nephews. He was the celebrity guest each family wanted for the holidays and special occasions. For the last 30 years of his life, Great Uncle Dan was affectionately known as "Gruncle Dan" by the family.*

Rick's second numinous experience in the house shows Dan's generous and helpful nature and came just days before the sale of the house actually closed. The night before closing, Rick swung by the house to see that everything looked alright. One of the requirements the lender had given for the sale was that the round portico on the front of the house be fixed. The contractor Rick hired to take care of the job had neglected to paint it after the repair. Nervous that the unpainted portico could cause a hiccup in the sale, Rick ran to the store to get paint, an electric spray painter and plastic. However, upon returning to the house, he realized he still faced a few problems (the outlet and the painter didn't match—three prongs vs. two—he'd forgotten to get something to cut the plastic and he couldn't reach the portico), so he decided to ask Dan Watson for a hand.

> *I stood in the front door, because at this point I was like, "Maybe it's haunted. I don't know. Maybe someone's here." Dan Watson was the last one that lived here. Everybody loved him. My parents loved him. He was the kindest person, wrote music....It didn't feel like a weird thing. It just kind of felt like a positive space. So I stand in the front door like, "Dan, I love your house. I'm going to protect it. I'm going to keep it. I just need help with three things. I need a ladder or stool so I can get high enough to paint the top. I need something to cut this plastic thing, and I need a way to get this electric spray painter to plug in somewhere....So then I walked through the front door into the kitchen, and next to the kitchen counter was a stool that was tall enough* [to reach the portico], *on the kitchen counter was a knife, like a letter opener knife that I still have...that was perfect for cutting the plastic. And then next to that was an extension cord with a converter from a three-prong to a two-prong...I was like, "Oh my goodness, this might be real." It was late, at least nine o'clock at night, totally dark. It was just me. But I was like, "That's incredible." And so it worked.*

It would seem that both Rick Atkin and Dan Watson wanted to ensure the transfer and restoration of the home went smoothly.

One of Rick's other haunting experiences involved seeing a handprint appear on the hardwood floor that he'd been restoring after removing the carpet. Much like Aaron Timm's experiences with Toquerville's woman in white, all of Rick's interactions with Dan seem positive. And this is not how we usually think of haunted houses. People don't flock to commercial haunted houses every October to feel warm and fuzzy or to get help with a home improvement project. Even the term *haunting* itself feels ominous and for good reason. It comes from the Latin *ominosus*, meaning "foreboding."

Sitting in the Watson house with Rick, I didn't sense anything close to foreboding. In fact, it was difficult not to notice the warmth and openness the home exudes. From the moment I stepped into it, the house felt welcoming. Some buildings do that. Whether it's the architecture, the lighting, the style and layout of the decor or something less measurable, something a bit more ethereal, some spaces just have more personality. One building feels cold and unwelcoming, while others make you feel like you could stay there forever.

As science writer Michael Bond points out in "The Hidden Ways That Architecture Makes You Feel," we know "that buildings and cities can affect our mood and well-being, and that specialized cells in the hippocampal region of our brains are attuned to the geometry and arrangement of the spaces we inhabit."[116] But can people and events also affect the way a space feels, even after they're gone? There are plenty who would argue that they can and do. In some cases, as with the ghost town of Grafton, the atmosphere of a space is most heavily impacted by the way we relate to it. For one person, a specific location, let's say a public park, could feel smothering if it's attached to a personal or family trauma. That same location could feel exhilarating for someone who had their first kiss there. Still, for someone else, it could be the aesthetics of the place that fills them with a sense of peace.

Homes aren't just any space, though. They are our personal sanctuaries. They are the heart of our families and the center of our lives. Our homes are a part of us, especially in America, where we've tied home ownership to our egos, our sense of status and the very identity of what our country is. As Colin Dickey notes:

> *In the United States, the most common—the most primal—haunted place is a house. Home ownership has always been intertwined with the American dream; we have magnified this simple property decision in part because it represents safety and security. The haunted house is a violation of this comfort, the American dream gone horribly wrong.*[117]

Here, though, we have a haunting that, perhaps, emphasizes how the American dream can go and stay right. A family home. An eccentric, gold-loving mayor who dedicated himself to his community. A son who took that home and opened it up to that community. A family who made that very personal space about more than themselves, and a man who uprooted his life to see that the home remains safe. These are pieces of a different kind of ghost story, a different kind of American story. I once had a student ask me how I'd define the American dream. Honestly, up to that point, I'd never given it much thought, but "The New Colossus," the poem inscribed on the Statue of Liberty, jumped into my mind. Specifically, the lines "Give me your tired, your poor / Your huddled masses yearning to breathe free, / The wretched refuse of your teeming shore. / Send these, the homeless, tempest-tost to me." I told him doing that, making a space where that poem holds true, is the American dream. I'd later get some of those lines tattooed on my arm.

The author giving a poetry performance on the front lawn of the Watson house. *Photo by Diana Frances.*

It's been a couple of years since Rick's last experience with Dan Watson. He said that it feels like Dan stuck around a little while just to make sure that he could trust him with the place. And Rick has shown him that he can. From consulting the family about renovation and addition plans to hosting community events in the front yard (as Rick said, "That was part of the intent behind [buying] the home: to protect that front yard and create a community space. That's why I do the music and that kind of stuff up there"), even picking gold every time he has to choose a metal fixture, Rick is doing everything he can to keep the spirit of Dan Watson and the Watson house alive, even if Dan himself has seen fit to move on.

Elaborating on the American haunted house, Dickey noted that "buried inside the word 'inhabit' is habit: a way of being, the patterns and repetitions of life." So while the typical haunted house may be formed around violence or tragedy, where these events have bled into the walls, maybe some haunted houses are shaped by other habits. Maybe they are imbued with sincerity and eccentricity. Maybe, just maybe, the habits of a kind and generous life can paint the walls of a home with something sublime, filling the space with a lasting and warm light.

CHAPTER 10

SKINWALKERS AND THE THEFT OF NATIVE AMERICAN BELIEFS

Sitting inside a thin nylon tent in the dead of winter, snuggled away in our sleeping bags, we stayed up well past the "lights out" order our Scout leaders had given us. We'd stuffed our shoes and clothes to the bottom of our bags, so that when we had to dress at the crack of dawn for a snowy hike, they would be warm. Illuminated by flashlights, shadows dancing around inside the tent, we took turns telling scary stories. I was the youngest in the tent and simply listened, wide-eyed, as the other boys told ghost stories, stories of monsters and murders. The air inside the tent was tense but not uncomfortable—as is usually the case during such late-night ghost story sessions. That is, until the oldest boy, probably fifteen or sixteen, asked the question that I've found causes people (in the Southwest, at least) to squirm more than any other supernatural question. *Have you ever heard of skinwalkers?*

I've had old, young, religious, skeptical, rich and poor people all show the same bodily shiver of discomfort when I switch the topic from ghosts or bigfoot to skinwalkers. The really interesting part? All of these people are non-Native and, overwhelmingly, they are white, while skinwalker lore is something belonging to the Navajo. I remember the way my skin grew tight as this boy told us that skinwalkers were Indians who'd made a deal with the devil for supernatural powers. They'd wear the skins of dead animals and hunt for live flesh. He told us a specific story about him and his brothers driving around out in the desert when, out of nowhere, they saw a man running alongside their truck. They sped up, and the man,

Above: Location of a skinwalker sighting near Gunlock reservoir.

Left: View of the night sky from Gunlock State Park, where several skinwalker sightings have taken place.

draped in a wolf hide, kept pace. Faster and faster they pushed, until the truck's speedometer was pinned. Still, the skinwalker stayed right next to them without even breaking a sweat. He even casually turned his head to give them a flash of his yellow eyes before suddenly vanishing. Nearly buried in my bag now, I whispered, "Why? Why did it stop?" Confidently, the boy replied, "Well, we were on sacred Indian ground. It chased us until we were out of its territory."

This story, and the way the boy told it, highlight a number of themes found in non-Native supernatural tales that deal with Natives or Native-related ideas. There are hordes of stories about cursed Native bones and cemeteries. Some of the most iconic horror films of all time are set in buildings or areas built on top of Native American burial grounds. The plot for the 1982 film *Poltergeist*, with its famous line "They're here," is based on a real estate development having been built on, and thus cursed by, a Native American burial ground. *Pet Cemetery* (1989), the 1979 film *The Amityville Horror*, even Jack Nicolson's *The Shining* (1980) involve or are set in these sacred Native spaces. All of these, and the majority of oral lore, hint at a deep and unacknowledged cultural guilt associated with American history as it deals with the country's Indigenous people. This idea can be traced back to the 1700s. As Colin Dickey notes, "The Anglo fascination with Indian burial lands stretches back at least to the eighteenth century. The Revolutionary poet Philip Freneau was one of the earliest to approach these sacred lands with a mix of exoticism and foreboding."[118] Under the banner of manifest destiny, westward expansion led to the deaths of millions of Indigenous people (outdated estimates say the number barely broke one hundred thousand, but most contemporary estimates put the number well into the millions).[119] In a horrifyingly real way, American history is the story of building on top of an Indigenous graveyard that we created, and we are haunted by that knowledge. Of course, one of the problems with this idea is that it paints Native Americans as a bygone race rather than a living people, a culture still fighting for survival. Sacred Native land is protected until we need to build a wall or an oil pipeline. But skinwalker lore, particularly non-Native skinwalker lore, can show us more than our guilt, especially when contrasted with actual Native lore (I use Native here in a broad sense, but as stated earlier, skinwalkers are specifically a Navajo belief).

In a Reddit post from September 2, 2018, a user identified as Lifeline2170 made a plea for advice after what they believed was an interaction with a skinwalker.

Possible skin walker experience in southern Utah 9-2-18. Might have been followed, please read and offer any advice/help.

So last night me and some friends went on a camping trip for my fiancé's 18th birthday. We went to the red cliffs desert reserve in St George, Utah. All night we had a very eerie feeling, but just wrote it off as being an hour out into the desert in the middle of the night. Throughout the night things kept getting more and more heated between us for reasons we didn't really understand. A guy who was with us and I went to go get firewood, and started chopping a dead limb off a tree, but I kept stopping because I was hearing stuff moving out of my field of vision, felt like I was in danger, felt I was being watched from at least two places, and got the feeling I needed to leave so I just stopped chopping the limb halfway through. The two dogs we had at one point started freaking out and we're terrified of something that was behind our tent, so we went and looked but didn't see anything so assumed it was just a coyote or some animal or something. Me and my fiancé are both empaths, and she's a medium and we have both had many supernatural experiences through our lives, and we knew something was wrong. We laid down in the tent and she nearly had a panic attack so we decided to sleep in a car instead of with everyone else. As soon as we got in the car, she broke down crying and couldn't explain why, so I chalked it up to stress or something. Eventually we both [fell] *asleep, and sometime between three and four in the morning I woke up because I had been having a dream that there were two witches around us that we couldn't see, but they were going to send creatures or something after us, and I woke up with a very bad feeling. I decided to try to sleep more when my fiancé sits up very suddenly and says "I keep hearing things. It sounds like there's girls talking and giggling so let's see if they're awake and maybe we can get the hell out of here." She then went to open the door but I had a very bad feeling and begged her not to, but as soon as she did, the voices stopped, the dogs weren't making noise (they are both attention whores and constantly whine), the coyotes we had been hearing since maybe 2:00 am, and even all the crickets that had been deafening all night were silent. So she closes the door, and the voices start again. Around 5:30 am, we see a light coming towards us and it's one of our friends who says she and another friend can't sleep and the dogs are freaking out and they want to leave, so we start comparing what's gone on the past few hours, and they had heard the voices too and thought it was us, so they almost left the tent to see if we wanted to leave but they felt like they shouldn't leave the tent. We* [packed] *up and* [left] *by 6:00 am, and something just didn't feel right. We go back around 10:30 am for*

Lightning storm in Red Cliffs Desert Reserve, where Lifeline2170 had their skinwalker experience.

> *some friends who decided to stay the whole time, and they say that after we left they kept hearing things walking around the tent, both small and quadrupedal but also large and bipedal, so they made noise until the things went away, then built the fire back up. We left officially around 11:00 am and didn't want to look back, and decided never to come back again, and* [we] *all felt a sense of relief when we finally made it through the hour-long trip back to a road. Now we think we might have been followed because home alone, we start hearing growling and other noises, as well as the tv in the living room turning on and off by itself. Does anyone have advice on what to do*[?][120]

Lifeline's fear and concern seem sincere, and this shows through in their interactions with commenters on their post. Their story hits on some common threads in skinwalker lore: feeling watched, hearing whispering, animals acting strange and hearing both quadra- and bipedal steps, though, each of those things could also easily apply to any number of other supernatural legends. More than the traditional skeptic's question of "Why interpret the physical details of the evening in a paranormal context?" we can and should ask the question, "Why interpret them in *this* paranormal context?"

Many cultures have some form of shapeshifting animalistic lore: European werewolves, Chinese *huli jing*, Japanese *kitsune*, Somali *qori ismaris* and the Slavic *veles*. So why the Navajo skinwalker? Why not the far more familiar lore of werewolves? Is it simply the proximity of a location to the origin of the lore? Looking closer, we can see that it is potentially much, much more.

Jessica T. shared her skinwalker experience with me. It is also set in the Southwest.

> *The ranch is about 2 hours from me. About 25 years ago my friends and I decided to take a road trip to Wyoming for fireworks and real beer. We decided while we were out there we were just going to camp out, drink, smoke and eat. I left camp to pee. I did my thing and went for a walk to finish a joint in my pocket. I saw a human boney face with yellow greenish eyes, but its ears were pointy and hairy and it* [had] *4 legs; the hind legs were longer* [than] *the front ones. It was breathing out mist. It looked at me. I looked at it. And it just walked by. And it smelled like death. I watched it till it left my sight. Ran back to my friends* [and] *told them what happened. Grabbed what I had with me and hitchhiked home.*

Jessica's story shows connections to other non-Native skinwalker lore. The story takes place away from home; however, the speaker isn't legend tripping. Jessica wasn't trying to have a spooky experience. This is an area where non-Native skinwalker lore differs from other common types of supernatural folklore. As I mentioned in the chapter on Grafton, there is a cycle where lore sparks legend tripping, which creates memorate, which then turn into new lore; however, with these stories, I've found it's rare to discover stories where the speaker was out hunting for skinwalkers or any other type of supernatural lore.

An interesting area where Jessica's story veers away from the majority of the non-Native skinwalker tales I've heard is that, like with the tale I heard as a Boy Scout, Jessica's narrative contains a good bit of detail. In both stories, we actually see the skinwalker. In Jessica's, we smell it.

Another non-Native skinwalker story comes to us from Ryan Redd, a twenty-four-year-old man from southeastern Utah. Sitting at an A&W in Logan, Utah, Ryan told his story to Jon Tanner, who recorded it for a folklore class at Utah State University. According to Jon, Ryan "told this story in an almost hushed tone as if it was some kind of personal secret he was telling [him]. It was obvious as he told the story that the thought of the occasion still spooks him a bit. After telling [Jon] about it he shuddered more than once and laughed nervously as if to shake off his nerves a little bit."

> *Back while I was in high school in Blanding* [in southeastern Utah] *I was out late cruising around town with a few of my buddies. We went down a long dirt road that cut straight into the desert and we were already starting to get pretty spooked because we were far away from town and it was pitch black. Most of the road was out in the open with low vegetation like sagebrush and stuff but after a while we got to a part where we could see a small clump of trees that* [completely] *surrounded the road. It just seemed weird because there weren't any other trees in* [sight]. *Anyway, we just continue to drive under the trees, we're riding in my own pickup, and suddenly there's a crazy loud slap on top of the truck. We of course squeal like girls and I peel out driving like crazy to get out of there. Later when we got back to town and were all still freaking out, we got out and looked at the top of the truck and there were long scratch marks like claws that left like 8 inch scratches from front to back. Scared the hell out of us. We were all sure that it was a skin walker in some shape.*[121]

Like with the other stories, there are some common elements to Ryan's encounter. That they were in a vehicle and that it was late at night is fairly consistent. Likewise, the discovery of some physical evidence—scratch marks—is also common. Most telling, however, is that all three of these stories take place away from "civilization." Ryan's takes place "down a long dirt road that cut straight into the desert…far away from town." Lifeline's story happens "an hour out into the desert" and Jessica's narrative is set "out there." These settings reflect a removal from the safety of modern society. They also demonstrate a motif common to non-Native lore where the speaker intentionally ventures out into the desert to escape from the mundane nature of modernity, for adventure, only to find something a little too "wild" out there. Wild, primitive, savage: all these ideas tie into harmful stereotypes of Indigenous people.

When we go into the desert, away from the safety of civilization, our minds start to reach out of the discomfort of the situation into latent cultural fears and biases. It is not a new idea that both American popular culture and folk culture have been heavily embedded with the notion that among the things we should fear in a savage landscape—when we're away from the safety of society, "outside the wagon circle"—are the Indigenous people we've been ingrained to see as equally savage. And where the threat of a "savage

Indian" raid doesn't hold much sway in a contemporary subconscious, the mysterious and frightening Indigenous lore of skinwalkers can. There is also something to the idea, in the versions of the lore involving vehicles, that our modern advancements are a last line of defense against the supernatural and/or the primitive.

The problem of seeing Indigenous peoples as savage is an idea that we discuss at length in my Academic Approaches to the Supernatural class. As non-Natives, we tend to lump the way we think about Native Americans into one of two categories. I call it the demon and the angel dilemma. On one side, we see Indigenous peoples as primate savages to be feared, pitied or improved. It's easy to trace where this notion has come from; it is nearly impossible to find a reference in political, historical or literary texts to Indigenous peoples that doesn't identify them as savage or primitive. Politicians used this negative stereotype as the basis for horrifying legislation like the Indian Removal Act of 1830, the General Allotment Act of 1887 and the Compulsory Indian Education Act of 1891. These pieces of legislation did unforgivable damage to Indigenous communities, damage that can still be felt today as tribes struggle to reclaim the religions, cultures and languages that they weren't legally able to practice until the passage of the American Indian Religious Freedom Act in 1978.

The flip side of this dilemma is viewing Natives as magical beings with a mystical connection to nature. This is the genesis of the new age movement. It is also the idea at the center of a majority of the appropriation and commodification of Native culture. It is easy to slip into arguing that this is okay because it is a positive portrayal of Indigenous people. However, as Native activist and scholar Adrienne Keene put it while discussing the issues of the Harry Potter series coming to America and incorporating Native stories and beliefs:

> *We fight so hard every single day as Native peoples to be seen as contemporary, real, full, and complete human beings and to push away from the stereotypes that restrict us in stock categories of mystical-connected-to-nature-shamans or violent-savage-warriors. Colonization erases our humanity, tells us that we are less than, that our beliefs and religions are "uncivilized," that our existence is incongruent with modernity. This is not ancient history, this is not "the past." The ongoing oppression of Native peoples is reinscribed everyday through texts and images like this....How in the world could a young person watch this and not make a logical leap that Native peoples belong in the same fictional world as Harry Potter?*[122]

She goes on to point out the very real problems this type of categorization has for Indigenous groups.

> *We are also fighting everyday for the protection of our sacred sites from being destroyed by mining, fracking, and other forms of "development." These sites are sacred. Meaning they have deep roots in our spiritual beliefs, hold sacred power, and connect us to our ancestors. If Indigenous spirituality becomes conflated with fantasy "magic"—how can we expect lawmakers and the public to be allies in the protection of these spaces?*

This is to say nothing of issues like the terrifying and horribly underreported trend of missing and murdered Indigenous women.

One of the issues Keene takes with the Potter series specifically is its inclusion of skinwalkers. Pop culture representation of the lore and legends of Indigenous peoples is problematic for many reasons. Whether it's the Navajo belief in skinwalkers or the Ojibwe belief in windigos, non-Native representation of these beliefs often strips them of their meaning. As Kallie Hunchman states in "Stolen Spirits: The Appropriation of the Windigo Spirit in Horror Literature":

> *Although well-documented in Western literature, the windigo spirits present in stories like Stephen King's* Pet Sematary *and Algernon Blackwood's "The Wendigo" are stripped of their original context and reduced to mere stereotypes of the cultures from which they originate.*[123]

Similarly, non-Native representations of skinwalkers miss the cultural context and the importance of the belief, often replacing it with simplified and harmful stereotypes. This idea of stripping the context and depth from an idea to make it simpler and more consumable applies well beyond the realm of Native appropriations. One of my favorite explorations of this idea is from Flannery O'Connor, discussing the oversimplification of Catholic beliefs. Specifically, in her example, she's looking at the over-sentimentalizing of the belief.

> *Sentimentality is a skipping of the process* [of redemption] *in its concrete reality and an early arrival at a mock state of innocence, which strongly suggests its opposite. Pornography, on the other hand, is essentially sentimental, for it leaves out the connection of sex with its hard purpose, and so far disconnects it from its meaning in life as to make it simply an experience for its own sake.*[124]

This pornography metaphor as well as the connection between O'Connor's Catholicism and Native appropriations seems like a stretch at first, but upon closer inspection, it highlights a complex and crucial point. The idea of disconnecting something from its meaning to make it "an experience for its own sake" is exactly what American culture has done, not just to windingos and skinwalkers but to nearly every consumable Native belief. When we turn windigos and skinwalkers into the stuff of monster movies and creature features, we don't just get the details wrong; we continue an assault on a culture that has been under constant barrage for over two hundred years. We turn a complex piece of a real, lived culture into a cheap trick at a haunted house. We turn beliefs that are central to individuals and communities into a sort of cultural pornography. This problem is compounded by the commercialization of a culture that is strongly anti-commercial. As Hunchman notes in her discussion of the windigo:

> *The appropriation of the windigo, like the appropriation of many Native American cultural ideas, is driven by a capitalistic appetite for money and fame. The irony of the appropriation of the windigo lies in the deep significance it holds in its Native communities as a warning against harmful and selfish appetites.*[125]

While not exactly the same, at least some part of the cultural significance of skinwalkers for Navajo communities lies in the idea of selfishness and greed for power.

One place where you can feel O'Connor's pornography metaphor really come to life in relation to the Navajo belief is in a local *St. George News* segment: "No Filter: Talking about Skinwalkers." As the video (which I show my students every year) starts, we see two bouncy non-Native hosts making goofy faces to a background of Native drum sounds. One host announces that they should go on an adventure. The other responds, "Growing up I used to hear tales and stories about these supernatural creatures called skinwalkers." Both men laugh before the other responds, "Whoa, I don't think you're even allowed to talk about them." After deciding to "get to the bottom of it," the hosts announce a giveaway associated with the segment. The giveaway involves viewers locating a number of Native arrowheads the two have hidden around the St. George area that people can find to win items like a sage stick, an Indian matchbox and an arrowhead necklace—all commodified pieces of Indigenous culture.

As the hosts interview a handful of locals about what they've heard or not heard in relation to the lore, again with goofy faces and laughs aplenty, we get another heavy dose of "You're not supposed to talk about them." This is neither delivered in a respectful way—say, the way the same team might mention that you're not supposed to talk about specific details of the LDS temple ceremony—nor in the way Natives actually believe that you shouldn't talk about skinwalkers—that to talk about them is to invite or attract them. As if to highlight this lack of respect and understanding, a graphic appears on screen of a Black Lives Matter protester with tape over their mouth—only the word *Black* has been covered over so the tape reads "Skinwalker Lives Matter."

One local woman does share a skinwalker story very similar to the one I heard as a Boy Scout, again emphasizing the vehicle motif. The men then talk to an eighty-nine-year-old Apache man who seems to have been brought on simply as a gag to play up the "We don't talk about them" bit rather than for any legitimate reason, as the brief clip shows him saying, "I told you, I know nothing, I have seen nothing."

The segment almost finds a moment of redemption as the hosts interview four-time world kickboxing champion Blackhawk Walters, who, despite the behavior of his hosts, shares some cultural insights. However, the two men show more respect for his kickboxing accomplishments than they do for the tradition and beliefs he shares with them. As Walters tells us "ten things that you probably never heard about skinwalkers," one host scratches his chin, wide-eyed, in comic interest before again displaying exaggerated faces and audible gasps at hearing some of the details Walters mentions. Meanwhile, the other host mostly stares off beyond the camera looking, honestly, bored. So, here, even though the information presented is culturally accurate—Walters makes the excellent point that there are "over 600 Indian tribes and [they] speak over 300 different languages" and that the details he shares only apply to his specific tribe and clan—the tone outweighs it, causing the segment to do nothing more than perpetuate a culture of disrespect and misunderstanding of Native Americans. To save you having to watch the segment, here are Blackhawk Walters's ten things:

1. All skinwalkers are evil.
2. A new skinwalker must carry the pelt of the animal they want to turn into.
3. They are also called shapeshifters, and when they change their form, they must turn into four-legged creatures.

4. To become the highest order of a skinwalker, they must kill a blood relative or a loved one.
5. Skinwalkers can manufacture any voice they want.
6. An advanced skinwalker doesn't need to carry a pelt to change into an animal.
7. If a skinwalker makes eye contact with you, it can freeze you in your tracks and steal your soul.
8. Never talk about a skinwalker at night.
9. If you hear strange noises outside your house, look out the window to make sure there are no strange animals outside.
10. You better have strong medicine if you run into a skinwalker.[126]

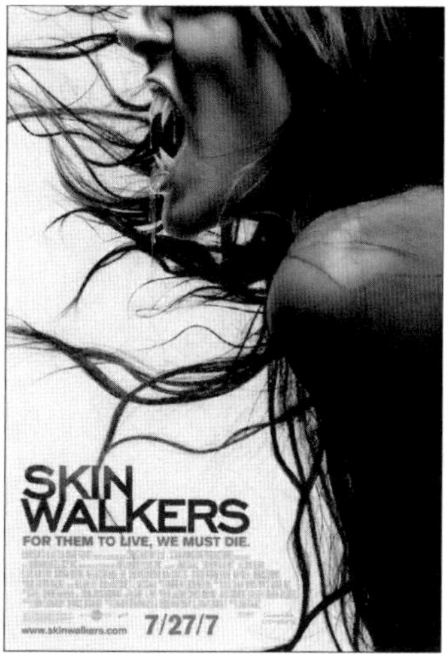

Poster for the film *Skinwalkers*. *Lionsgate.*

Beyond cheesy local news segments, this trend can be seen in films like the 2006 film *Skinwalkers*. While the film starts off by using the correct Navajo term for skinwalker, it quickly veers into a movie that feels like a rebranded werewolf flick. With the exception of a short bit by actor Tom Jackson, the film has no actual Native representation. Not that they tried to pass non-Native actors off as Natives; rather, the script simply removes Natives from the lore. Instead, the story focuses on a family line of white people who have picked up the skinwalker "curse." And in what seems like an attempt to jump the cultural ignorance and insensitivity shark, the key plot point is that the family's son is the "chosen one" who can break the curse. Yes, the white boy is the only one who can end the Native curse.

While examining offensive and inaccurate representation of skinwalker lore can demonstrate the many areas for improvement American culture still has when it comes to Indigenous peoples, when we look at non-Native and Native skinwalker stories side by side, we can see a variety of additional cultural truths.

Alexis Small grew up on the reservation in a primarily traditional Diné (Navajo) home. Speaking with me one afternoon, she related a series of skinwalker experiences she'd had. The first one took place when she was eight years old.

We lived by this huge dead volcanic peak close to Monument Valley.... We lived in a trailer. It was a single wide trailer. So, back then my mother and I would sleep in the living room on Friday nights, it was just like a family thing...My brothers were sleeping on the couch, my [sister's family] *were asleep in the other room, and my* [cousin's family] *were in the farthest room in the back.*

I just wake up to a big boom. And so I sit up and then you hear the boom again. It was right by the living room window. It jumped onto the roof and it ran the length of the trailer from one end to the other. Then it ran back down and jumped again. I hear it land, and you hear the dogs just going crazy. And [there] *was a man's voice in Navajo saying really disgusting things to my mom, and then it growls, and it runs off again, and it hits the other side of the trailer. And everyone by this point is in the living room. We're all scared. We're all wondering what's going on. The two older guys and my brother who's a year older than me, those three go outside. When you live out on the reservation in the rural areas, you absolutely have to have a gun. So they took the gun and went outside. They* [also] *take out there, one of them has an eagle feather, the other two had arrow heads—that's to protect themselves. So they went out and they came in and they said the thing was gone.*

An "Indian" Halloween costume. *Pixabay.*

One difference between the typical non-Native story and Alexis's is the setting. In non-Native skinwalker lore, the speaker has to step out of their typical life to engage with the lore. Alexis's story taking place at home emphasizes that this lore isn't something apart from her (Navajo) life but rather part of it. Likewise, the way Alexis's story is interwoven with other elements of Navajo belief (arrowheads, the Navajo language) demonstrates that the idea of skinwalkers isn't something that can be plucked from Native culture and transplanted into American pop culture without damaging both the lore and the culture it has been severed from.

Over the next couple of years, Alexis saw skinwalkers in the form of a wolf and, on a different occasion, in the form of a bear. She noted that in both instances, the skinwalkers had the appearance of the animal, but something was not quite right. Something was off. Their forms are a perversion of nature and the connection between man and animal.

At ten years old, while hanging out with her sister's boyfriend's sister, a little over an hour from her parents' house, Alexis had her most intense experience yet:

> *This was at dusk, and she and I went out to go feed the goats, we're just little kids…and we're carrying these big bowls of milk…*
>
> *We were talking, and then the dogs started barking. And we were just joking because, you know, we're thinking it's the evening, there's still some sunlight.…The sun was just above the ridge of the mountain. So we started joking, teasing each other, saying it's probably a Yanni. That's what we call* [skinwalkers]*, but it's called Yee Naaldlooshii in our language. For short we say Yanni, and like, even now, joking we'll be like, "Where did you yanni off to?"—meaning, like, where did you go? Where did you run off to? Where did you disappear to? But Yanni means "the thing is there one minute and then it's gone the next," so it's just a term we use.*
>
> *We just started laughing. But then the dogs really started barking, and* [her family] *had a lot of dogs mind you, because they had livestock. All of the sudden, all the dogs took off running behind us.*
>
> *There's a windmill maybe a quarter of a mile from the house. You could see* [the windmill] *on the hill, and the dogs took off running there. We were like, "Okay, let's not joke about it. Let's hurry up and get these goats fed."*
>
> *So we're trying to hurry up and feed them, and then the dogs came running back. And they were barking, barking. And then, on my peripheral on the right side, I saw…I saw this white thing go running between two trees that were there.…I thought it was one of the dogs, but then it clicks in my mind, like, "Dogs can't move that fast." So I turn and look at her, 'cause she's standing on my left. Her eyes got big, and she goes, "Run!"*
>
> *We were carrying the milk, and we just took off running. The ground isn't even. It's hard-packed sand, so it's very uneven. And literally the back of my hair stood up because I could feel this thing right behind us. So she's yelling as we're running. She's yelling for her brothers. And I trip on one of the little lumps, and I went falling—spilt the milk everywhere, fell in it, you know—so, I'm getting up trying to get the mud off of me from the milk, and I heard it right behind me and then…the smell! Those things, they smell like something dead because they use the skin of the dead animal, so they smell like death, like rotting…I just felt it right behind me, and the smell was so strong, and it was growling like a rabid dog. You could hear*

This page: Monument Valley Navajo Tribal Park.

it inhale and growl, and then you could hear the saliva in its mouth, and I was frozen. I couldn't move.

My nickname, it's my Navajo name, but the short end of it is Muzi.... I see my sister's boyfriend and his brothers come out, and they go, "Muz, run!" And I was trying to get my feet to move, and I couldn't. Then I just remembered them shooting—but not at me. And I heard the bullet go by, and then I was able to move, and I started running.

I get inside, and they're telling me to put ash on from the fireplace. That's another way to protect yourself (they even say put ash on your vehicle when you travel far), but I put ash on, and we lock the doors. And then the guys come back in, and they were putting ashes on the bullet. They were putting ashes on the gun. And so they said, "Lock the door behind us!" and they went back out, and you just hear gunfire everywhere, and then the front door started jiggling. So one of the older sisters, she was going to go open the door, but the mother yelled at her, and they all speak Navajo, but they're yelling at her and telling her not to open the door. And: "Just wait, just wait till they say something, and if it's one of them." And then she started calling to her sons, saying, "Is that you? Is that you? Is that you?" And they weren't answering, but the door kept jiggling. Then you hear gunfire. Then you hear all three of the guys' voices over on the left side, 'cause they were running up to the front porch. They came to the door. Whatever that was that was jiggling, it was trying to get in. So they came up to the front, and they were telling us, "Don't open the door! Don't open the door!" And then you hear more gunfire. And then they all came back in, and the mother put up Cedar and everybody blessed themselves. So that was probably one of the scariest things I've ever experienced.

I noted in an earlier chapter that supernatural lore "in the contemporary oral tradition is only slightly dramatic."[127] It's a door swinging open on its own. It's an object not being where you left it, or the vague feeling of someone watching you. Your hair standing up on end is the only proof of the supernatural. Here, in Alexis's story, her hair standing up on end is the least dramatic element of the story. In fact, listening to Alexis's story feels closer to listening to a bit of true crime, a story of a mugging or some other human-based threat. And that is one of the biggest differences between the non-Native and the Native skinwalker stories. For non-Natives, skinwalkers are otherworldly beings, supernatural monsters. For Natives, skinwalkers are a human threat. It's closer to someone telling the story of a drive-by shooting than a haunting.

Alexis's last pair of stories highlight this human element of the skinwalker lore. They demonstrate how the true horror of skinwalkers is closer to a family member trying to recruit you into a cult than a monster trying to eat you alive. They take place later in her life, when she was in junior high.

> *I had developed insomnia. So what I would do is, I would read as much as I can to try and* [get] *my eyes tired and whatnot....I guess I fell asleep while I was reading, but it was just before I had to get up to go to school....I fell asleep, and in my head, I don't remember what I was dreaming...I just heard this lady in my ear. She said "You think you can stop me? You think you can stop me?" She started screaming! When I woke up, my ears were ringing. And I heard...a loud thud, like somebody had jumped off the roof and then I heard—it sounds like hoofprints, like a horse, like a horse running, because it's heavy, it was a heavy sound. But instead of the four sounds you hear when a horse is galloping or running, it was only two. I could only count two feet or two hooves, and it ran from the west side to the east. I sat up, and I had my lights still on, and I was thinking, "It can see me through the window." So I immediately closed the curtains, and I turned my light off. I was so scared. My heart was pounding, and I was getting, you know, I was actually sweating...Just then, the alarm goes off. I would get up at 5:00 a.m. every morning to get ready to get on the bus by 6:00 just to get to school by 8:00, right?...*
>
> *My mom says that by 5:00 a.m. only good blessings come, but before 5:00 a.m., from midnight to then, bad things can happen. So I was just thinking, you know, "Thank God it's 5:00," because I don't know how long I was laying there scared....*
>
> *Then walking home from school in the evening when it's dusk, something was calling my name. It was like a whisper, but it was loud, and then something was throwing rocks at me....It was about a half a mile from the bus stop....It's a rural area, you get dropped off at the roadside and I'll have to...walk uphill...and something was calling my name, and I was told you don't answer, don't answer. You don't turn around. You don't look. And so rocks were being thrown at me as I was walking, and I have to hurry up and rush home without* [being] *scared, you know, not trying to show fear, trying to be brave.*

These types of experiences, hearing and seeing things, were the start of a much bigger issue for Alexis. As she explained to me, they were a sign of someone reaching out to her, trying to pull her toward the evil side of her gifts. That's what sits at the center of skinwalker lore: perversion of gifts or talents. Alexis elaborated on this idea as she described how her experiences came to a head later that year.

> *It's usually the people who learn these things* [the dark things] *have a gift....It's a medicine man, or a medicine woman, and you have different types of them. You have the crystal gazers, the hand tremblers and the ones who do the sand paintings, you know, they use things from the earth to heal. And way back when this thing started, being able to take the skin of an animal and use it, it was meant to use the spirit of that animal to heal, to protect the tribe. And what these people did is they took that ability, that gift, and they turned it evil....*
>
> *I have the hand trembling. That was transferred down through my mother's side, which is Navajo. My father, however, is Sioux, but my mother is Navajo, and on her side of the family they have the healing gifts.... When I was a teenager, I started dabbling in things like, I guess you could say the Wiccan type of witchcraft. And what I did, not knowing that I had a gift, was I opened up myself to things. I opened myself up [for] bad things to happen to me, and I was hearing things and seeing things.*
>
> *[It was] skinwalkers that were coming to my parents' home, and they were around my parents' home, trying to take me, like an initiation, into what they were doing. In order to do that, they physically had to take me, and it was like going into a trance almost.*
>
> *Because I was having all these things happen as a teen. I was very angry. I was always angry. And I had this big fight with my mom...and...I walked out at night into the woods....I was just going to go sit somewhere and just calm down, and then I hear a truck...down in the wash. So I was standing there looking, I could see the headlights, and then all of a sudden I heard, it was so weird, it sounded like the Navajo language, but it was just twisted around somehow, and then I see two men and a lady. And they were dressed not like you would expect—you know,* [the] *modern way, the way we dress now—but they were in their traditional clothing. And the lady, I just remember her walking in front of me, maybe about two yards, and... she was going over the vegetation and I was expecting to hear the crunch 'cause she was stepping in bushes, and there was no crunch. There was no sound, and that was it. I just blacked out.*
>
> *The* [next] *thing I remember...I'm walking towards my parents' home in the complete opposite* [direction] *of where I had walked out into the woods. As I get closer, I immediately just start vomiting. And then*

> *I had a bloody nose, and my stepdad ran inside, and he got, you know, when you're cleaning ash you have like that little shovel, he used that to get ash and he brought it outside....(People think that you burn sage to clear your home. Us, we don't burn sage, we burn cedar* [leaves]....*So you put that in the four directions, and then you make a circle, and then you bless yourself with that)....He brought the ashes out, and he told me, "Don't do it out here, you come inside, and you have to bless yourself." So* [what] *I was told, after we had a ceremony for me, is that what happened was that those people, I knew who they were. And they were trying to teach me things 'cause of my gift, they wanted to exploit it. So, they wanted to use me to make themselves powerful.*

Alexis's story contains some of the elements Blackhawk Walters noted. She heard strange noises outside her house, the skinwalker was able to "freeze her in her tracks" (she blacked out) and she needed "strong medicine" to deal with the aftereffects of the encounter.

When contrasting her experience with non-Native lore and pop culture, one of the most interesting things to stand out is the presence and purpose of the vehicle. In the non-Native lore, the vehicles separate the speaker from the skinwalker. It is a last bit of civilization that saves the speaker from the beast; however, in Alexis's story, the truck is what brings the skinwalkers to her. This, in part, demolishes the civilization vs. wild/primitive/savage motif and should cause non-Natives to reconsider their definition of civilization.

Above all else, the thing that sticks with me after listening to many Indigenous people share their beliefs and culture is how complex and different these beliefs are from the western Christian culture that tried to

Hovenweep National Monument.

Frozen waterfall on Best Friends Animal Sanctuary property. Best Friends' property is rumored to have had several skinwalker sightings.

erase them, the culture most of us who might try to understand Native beliefs come from. There is no shortcut to understanding Indigenous people and their beliefs. They are built on a structure the very foundation of which requires a drastic paradigm shift to understand. On top of that, there are subtle nuances from tribe to tribe.

Alexis's experience and her comments elaborate on how skinwalkers are not monsters nor, as I'd heard as a Boy Scout, Natives who "made a deal with the devil." Instead, they are Navajo who have perverted the gifts they have been given. They are real people. As Alexis noted, "Those people, I knew who they were." This fits with the tone and details other Navajo individuals have told me. Skinwalker lore, for a Navajo, seems to be more about a darkness within one's community, with people they know, than with a strange mythical monster.

For non-Natives, our skinwalker lore highlights a different darkness in our community, a darkness born from past prejudices and crimes, the effects of which have crept through our history to nestle quietly in the shadows of our worldview. They whisper to us about savages. They claw at our empathy, tearing down the understanding we could be building for another culture. They cause our image of that culture to shapeshift into something far less complex, less beautiful and less real than it is.

CHAPTER 11

ODDS AND ENDS

Each chapter of this book has explored lore attached to a particular theme or location. To do this takes more space than just telling the stories that are part of that lore. Between research that establishes the historical framework and presenting the ideas of folklorists, scientists and writers (along with my own reflections and ideas), a full chapter, done the way I felt they needed to be done, requires a lot of space.

What follows are bits of lore that didn't fit the space allotted or the format chosen. Some, like the smoking head of Mountain Meadows, just didn't fit in their chapter. Others, like the collection of narratives from Mexican Hat, I desperately wanted to explore in a full chapter but, again, couldn't due to lack of space. Lastly, there are stories, like the haunted Denny's, that I couldn't find enough material on to flesh the lore out.

The Talking Head of Mountain Meadows

From Austin E. Fife's "Popular Legends of the Mormons":

My mother's sister Elizabeth lived in southern Utah, and she and her husband were coming up here and they passed the place where the Mountain Massacre had been—in that vicinity. They camped just a short distance from where that tragedy had occurred, and they built a fire and cooked supper, and were sitting around the campfire after supper, and looked over where that tragedy had happened and saw a man's head coming out of the ground and it just slowly and gradually came out of the ground and smoked a pipe. That was supposed to be the devil.[128]

Ghostly Mother in Escalante

It didn't make it into the chapter because it felt too off topic, but in researching the curse of Escalante Petrified Forest, someone mentioned lore about a house on Main Street in Escalante that is haunted by the ghost of a mother rocking her crying child to sleep.

Fort Pearce

While there were never battles fought at Fort Pearce, I did encounter two people who noted that they'd heard phantom screams and gunshots in the area, as well as feeling that they were being watched.

Haunted Denny's

I really wanted this one to work out, but after polling the community and speaking to several employees, the manager and the owner, there simply wasn't enough there. However, a few people did mention that the Denny's on Main Street near Bluff Street in St. George is haunted. They mentioned former employees telling stories of dishes flying across the kitchen and of customers talking to phantom servers.

Shivwits Cemetery

Some people reported feeling an ominous presence in the cemetery (this ties in to the point made about Native American burial sites in the skinwalkers chapter). And one person shared a story about seeing something fly at their car while hanging out at the cemetery.

GUNLOCK RESERVOIR

There are some vague accounts of skinwalkers and phantom "Native" drumming at Gunlock. There is lore that pioneers tossed the bodies of murdered Natives into the reservoir. The most detailed story regarding Gunlock is about a spectral Native hitchhiker dressed in white who seems to stay fixed in your rearview mirror even as you drive farther past her.

LEEDS CEMETERY

This small cemetery is lovely in the daytime and a perfect atmosphere for spooky encounters after dark. People have shared stories of dark figures lurking at the corner of their vision, and I heard at least one tale of the cemetery's iron gate opening and closing on its own and another of sudden and drastic temperature drops.

MINES

Southern Utah has a number of old mines, most notably at Silver Reef and near the Leeds Cemetery, which are understandably closed off from the public for safety concerns. While I couldn't find anything specific, several people made reference to there being stories of ghostly miners haunting the tunnels.

THE HARDY HOUSE

This pioneer home located in Ancestor Square in St. George has been everything from a restaurant to a real estate office and a Mystery Escape

Room. Most of the lore is just vague references to the building being haunted. The story that I heard with the most detail dealt with Sheriff Hardy (whom the house once belonged to) being shot at in the house by miners from Silver Reef. According to the Washington County Historical Society website:

> *Perhaps the most famous, or infamous, moment in Hardy's law-enforcement career came when an accused murderer from Silver Reef was brought to St. George to await trial. Infuriated vigilante miners came that night, broke into the house, overpowered the sheriff and his helpers, took the keys to the jail, and strung the miscreant to a tree a block or so down the street. Sheriff Hardy never got over the fact that a prisoner was taken from him. During this incident, the house was slightly remodeled by a bullet and that bullet hole is still seen in one of its upstairs doors.*[129]

Kanab

In addition to a lack of the space needed to cover it, the reason Kanab didn't get a chapter had to do with a lack of new information and how much coverage the primary lore for the area has already received. While there are a number of references online, and in talking to locals, of skinwalker encounters on the property owned by Best Friends Animal Sanctuary, the most prominent lore in the area deals with Montezuma's treasure.

The tale of Freddie Crystal rolling into town with a treasure map that suggested Montezuma's legendary treasure had been buried near Kanab has been told everywhere from local newspaper articles to treasure hunter websites and the History Channel's *America Unearthed*. There are even a number of books on the subject, including one by Stephen Shaffer titled *Treasure of the Ancients*, published by Cedar Fort Press, which has had serious accusations of

This lake is said to hold Montezuma's treasure.

The Parry Lodge in Kanab is one of several haunted hotels in the town.

plagiarism leveled at it by J. Golden Barton at the Ancient Historical Research Foundation symposium held at Brigham Young University on May 25, 2005.[130] Despite sending several emails to Cedar Fort Press, I didn't receive a response.

After Freddie came into town in 1912, the entire community of Kanab joined in on the treasure hunt. There was a great article about the town's treasure hunt published in the *Saturday Evening Post* back in 1949.[131] While the hunt did turn up several Indigenous sites, it didn't turn up any treasure. That could have been the end of the story, if it hadn't been for Brandt Child, who believed the treasure actually sat in a different canyon "10 miles to the west—at the bottom of an algae-green pond."[132] The canyon, Three Lakes Canyon, had several stone carvings that led Child to believe the treasure sat in a secret chamber inside one of the lakes. After purchasing the land around one of the lakes, Child made several attempts to find the treasure but was deterred each time by "the curse." According to Child, divers he'd hired to explore the lake felt people pulling at them under the water, and one even had their respirator yanked out of their mouth. The land, after passing to Child's son, has since become the property of Best Friends Animal Sanctuary.

In the History Channel show on the curse, Stephen Shaffer tries to explain how the stone carvings show the treasure is buried in Three Lakes; however, while the mysterious symbol that both he and Child reference is an Indigenous symbol, academics have soundly rejected any connection between it and Montezuma's treasure. Among the more academically plausible interpretations is that the symbols are a water-mapping system to help the nomadic peoples locate water in the harsh desert. Kaye Feather Robinson, whose story I share in the Grafton chapter, co-published an article on the symbol that does a solid job of covering the various theories.[133]

As a side note to this side note, I heard a handful of haunted hotel stories while researching the curse in Kanab but did not have the space or time to adequately explore them.

St. George Tunnels

There are two tunnels with supernatural lore worth mentioning. The more established lore deals with the old Bigelow Tunnel. According to the Washington County Historical Society:

> *The Bigelow Tunnel was dug as part of the Highway 91 construction. According to National Surface Transportation Policy and Revenue Study Commission it had an hourly traffic of 585 vehicles in 1948. Sometime before 1954, a cut was made through the mesa and the highway was rerouted along the more level route. The tunnel was no longer on the main route, but may have still been used as an alternate route for a while. Sometime around 1970, the cut was widened and Highway 91 was replaced with I-15. The road running through the Washington Tunnel was eventually taken out of service. The tunnel still exists, but now is used for storage.*

The author and his son in front of the Nisson Park tunnel.

There is broadly shared lore that the tunnel is haunted, but I couldn't find an origin story or any specific memorate associated with it.

The other tunnel, located at Nisson Park in Washington City, is newer and not as broadly shared, but it has ties to an actual tragedy. The tunnel, which I used to take my son to look for ducks in, is said to be haunted by the ghost of a teen who hanged themselves from the tunnel. In looking for memorate and FOAF narratives involving the tunnel, I had several people message me about a very real tragedy involving a suicide near the tunnel. This is an example of supernatural lore birthing from an event the community might be uncomfortable talking about in more direct terms.

Silver Reef

If you'd asked me, when I first moved to Southern Utah in 2010, which location would most likely be filled with ghost stories, I'd have guessed Silver Reef. The mining town has a rich history filled with bar brawls and shootouts, and a number of "ghost hunters" have investigated the area, but surprisingly, there is little to no supernatural lore associated with Silver

Old bank at Silver Reef.

Sunset at Silver Reef.

Silver Reef Jail.

Reef. I did interview one ghost hunter who said they'd captured the voice of a Native boy on EVP equipment. However, aside from that—and a fun adventure with my son where we tried to catch ghosts with a trap made out of a shoebox and a stick, using french fries for bait—there isn't much supernatural going on out at Silver Reef. Now, that is not to say that there isn't anything going on at Silver Reef. The ghost town has been beautifully preserved and restored. Its history is fascinating and can be explored at the Silver Reef Museum and experienced through live reenactments, all thanks to the Silver Reef Foundation.

MEXICAN HAT

When I pulled into Mexican Hat, I was not impressed. It's situated just north of Monument Valley, and I'd booked a hotel to stay there as I explored the area, but an internet outage had nearly the whole town closed down. After a twenty-minute adventure with me and the hotel's receptionist trying to

The rock formation for which the town Mexican Hat is named.

figure out how I would pay for and check in to my room, I decided to try and get something to eat. Fortunately—yes, I said fortunately—the only place I could find open was the Swingin' Steak, which cooked me the best steak I have ever had in my life. And that heavenly piece of meat wasn't even the highlight of my meal. As I sat around the outside bar, I got to listen to my server Cody, the cook and a delightful older gentleman share local lore ranging from floating orbs to the Dark Canyon screamers and the Goat Man of Brown's Canyon.

The Dark Canyon screamers are linked to an old mining town, or a couple of mining structures, that got ruined by flooding, but people would stay out there still, and they'd hear "a big creature that screamed and sometimes made sounds like a baby crying."

The Goat Man of Brown's Canyon is basically what it sounds like: a goat… man. According to Cody, the goat man is an eight-foot-tall, muscular creature with the torso of a man and the legs and head of a goat. One day, while partying in the canyon with friends, Cody believes he may have stumbled upon the goat man's cave.

Mexican Hat also has many sightings of spirit orbs. I would actually love to do something bigger with Mexican Hat in the future.

NOTES

Introduction

1. Colin Dickey, *Ghostland: An American History in Haunted Places* (New York: Viking, 2016), 2.
2. Diane E. Goldstein, Sylvia Ann Grider and Jeannie Banks Thomas, *Haunting Experiences: Ghosts in Contemporary Folklore* (Logan: Utah State University Press, 2007), 60.
3. The Modern Rogue, "How Ghost Hunting TV Shows Trick You (And Themselves)," https://www.youtube.com/watch?v=IXu7tXixrtQ.
4. Chet Raymo, *Skeptics and True Believers: The Exhilarating Connection Between Science and Spirituality* (London: Walker Books, 1998), 2.
5. Peter Monaghan, "The Surprising Online Life of Legends," *Chronicle of Higher Education,* December 12, 2011.

Chapter 1

6. Wes Larsen, "Historic Buildings Along Toquer Boulevard," https://cdn-west.sqhk.co/cityoftoquerville/5d7igSi/walkingtourHistoric.pdf.
7. City of Toquerville website, https://www.toquerville.org.
8. Ibid.
9. Ibid.
10. Goldstein, Grider and Thomas, *Haunting Experiences*, 153.

11. National Register of Historic Places, https://www.nps.gov/subjects/nationalregister/index.htm.
12. Mary Phoenix, *Historic Buildings of Washington County*, vol. 2. (1992), 25.
13. Mark Doty, *Still Life with Oysters and Lemon* (Boston, MA: Beacon Press, 2002), 10.
14. Ageneta Grimby, "Bereavement among Elderly People: Grief Reactions, Post-Bereavement Hallucinations and Quality Of Life," *Acta Psychiatrica Scandinavica* 87, no. 1 (1993): 72–80. doi:10.1111/j.1600-0447.1993.tb03332.

Chapter 2

15. Yvar Mikhashoff, "Seymour, John Laurence," Oxford Music Online, Oxford University Press, December 1, 1992.
16. Abigail Wyatt, "Four Ghosts That Haunt Campus Year Round," *T-Bird Nation Blog*, October 25, 2016, https://www.suu.edu/blog/2016/10/spooky-ghost-stories.html.
17. Mikhashoff, "Seymour, John Laurence."
18. Glen Nelson, "Digging Up the Pasha's Garden," Mormon Artists Group, http://www.mormonartistsgroup.com/mormon_artists_group/Pasha.html.
19. Olin Downes, "New Native Opera Is Produced Here; 'In the Pasha's Garden,' by John L. Seymour, Sung by Cast Mostly American," *New York Daily News*, January 25, 1935.
20. Nelson, "Digging Up the Pasha's Garden."
21. Ibid.
22. Wyatt, "Four Ghosts."
23. Southern Utah University, "SUU Hauntings," *SUU Bird Book 2016–2017*, https://issuu.com/suuwebservices/docs/birdbookebook_pages.compressed.
24. "The Spirits of Old Main at Southern Utah University," Backpackerverse.com, https://backpackerverse.com/southern-utah-university/
25. "Ghost Story Errata," *Iron County Today*, March 2, 2010.
26. *SUU Bird Book 2016–2017*.
27. Darren M. Edwards, "The Uncomfortable Relationship between Sex and Violence in America" *Southern Utah Independent* (St. George, UT), March 1, 2016.
28. Goldstein, Grider and Thomas, *Haunting Experiences*, 86.

29. Adele Park, "'We Saw a Shadow Walk By': The Haunting of Southern Utah University," *Cedar City (UT) News*, October 29, 2021.
30. *SUU Bird Book 2016–2017.*
31. Dickey, *Ghostland*, 62.
32. "The Spirits of Old Main."
33. Tom Braun, "The Haunting of Old Main," *Thunderbird* (Cedar City, UT), October 28, 1986.
34. Jana Hassatt, "Old Main Fire," *Homestead Telegraph*, August 13, 2015, https://frontierhomestead.org/homestead-telegraph/2015/08/13/old-main-fire.
35. Dickey, *Ghostland*, 8.

Chapter 3

36. Utah DNR State Parks, https://stateparks.utah.gov.
37. Escalante Petrified Forest State Park visitors brochure.

Chapter 4

38. "Building the St. George L.D.S. Temple, A Holy Temple in St. George 1871–1877 A Miracle of Its Time," St. George Temple Visitors' Center, http://www.stgeorgetemplevisitorscenter.info/temple/buildingtemple.html.
39. Richley H. Crapo, "Grass-Roots Deviance from Official Doctrine: A Study of Latter-Day Saint (Mormon) Folk-Beliefs," *Journal for the Scientific Study of Religion* 26.4 (1987): 465–85.
40. Quoted in kirtland r.m., "...We Cannot Move the Foundation. This Spot Was Dedicated by the Nephites. Brigham Young," LDS Freedom Forum, https://www.ldsfreedomforum.com/viewtopic.php?p=1268583.
41. "St George—A Nephite Temple," Book of Mormon Evidence, December 5, 2019, https://bookofmormonevidence.org/st-george-a-nephite-temple/.
42. Boyd K. Packer, *The Holy Temple* (Salt Lake City, UT: Bookcraft, 1980).
43. James Edward Talmage, *The House of the Lord: A Study of Holy Sanctuaries, Ancient and Modern* (Salt Lake City, UT: Deseret News, 1912).
44. Brian H. Stuy, "Wilford Woodruff's Vision of the Signers of the Declaration of Independence," *Journal of Mormon History* 26, no. 1 (2000), 64–90, http://www.jstor.org/stable/23288590.
45. Mary B. Nicolini, "Is There a FOAF in Your Future," *English Journal* 78, no. 8 (December 1989).

46. Goldstein, Grider and Thomas, *Haunting Experiences*, 67.
47. Ibid., 146.
48. Brigham Young, *The Teachings of President Brigham Young: Vol. 3 1852–1854*, ed. Fred C. Collier (Salt Lake City, UT: Colliers).
49. Utah Legislative Assembly, *Journals of the Legislative Assembly of the Territory of Utah […]*, vol. 1, 1852.
50. Your Mormon Auntie, "Mormonism and the Paranormal: Are LDS Folks Afraid of Ghosts," *Southern Utah Independent* (St. George, UT), October 22, 2017.
51. Eric A. Eliason, "Spirit Babies and Divine Embodiment: PBEs, First Vision Accounts, Bible Scholarship, and the Experience-Centered Approach to Mormon Folklore," *BYU Studies Quarterly* 53, no. 2 (2014): 27.

Chapter 5

52. Richard F. Weingroff, "U.S. 666: 'Beast of a Highway'?" U.S. Department of Transportation Federal Highway Administration, https://www.fhwa.dot.gov/infrastructure/us666.cfm.
53. "Gov. Martinez Announces $78 Million Funding for U.S. Route 491," Navajo Nation press release, March 26, 2014, https://www.navajo-nsn.gov/Archived_Webpages_News_Releases/2014/mar14.html.
54. "NM History: Route 666, The Devil's Highway," *Roosevelt Review* (blog), October 22, 2019, https://www.therooseveltreview.com/nm-history-route-666-the-devils-highway/.
55. James T. Yenckel, "Refrains of Spain," *Washington Post*, December 29, 1991.
56. Weingroff, "U.S. 666."
57. Jodi Wilgoren, "The End of the Road For 'Devil's Highway,'" *New York Times*, June 13, 2003.
58. Robert H. Keller and Michael F. Turek, *American Indians and National Parks* (Tucson: University of Arizona Press, 1998), 37–38.
59. Ute Mountain Ute Tribe, https://www.utemountainutetribe.com.
60. "Native American Legends from Mountain Landscapes Nationwide," *Deseret News* (Salt Lake City, UT), June 16, 2010, https://www.deseret.com/2010/6/16/20121732/native-american-legends-form-mountain-landscapes-nationwide.
61. Jackie Krogmeier, "Native American Culture: Not for Sale," *Purdue Historian* 8, no. 1 (2017), https://docs.lib.purdue.edu/puhistorian/vol8/iss1/7.

62. American Indian Religious Freedom Act, 42 U.S.C. § 1996.
63. Laurance D. Linford, *Navajo Places: History, Legend, Landscape* (Salt Lake City: University of Utah Press, 2000), 264–65.
64. Krogmeier, "Native American Culture."
65. Lyra Radford, "10 Freaky Stories and Urban Legends That Prove Utah Is the Creepiest State," Ranker.com, updated September 23, 2021, https://www.ranker.com/list/creepy-utah-stories-legends/lyra-radford.
66. Linda Dunning, *Lost Landscapes* (Springville, UT: Cedar Fort, 2006).
67. Henry George Liddell and Robert Scott, *A Greek-English Lexicon* (Oxford: Clarendon Press, 1940).
68. Jeremy Black and Anthony Green, *Gods, Demons and Symbols of Ancient Mesopotamia: An Illustrated Dictionary* (London: British Museum Press, 1992).
69. Chris Ghan, "The Daevas in Zoroastrian Scripture" (master's thesis, University of Missouri–Columbia, 2014), 5
70. Black and Green, *Gods, Demons and Symbols.*
71. Dorian Gieseler Greenbaum, *The Daimon in Hellenistic Astrology* (Leiden: Brill, 2015), 129, https://doi.org/10.1163/9789004306219.
72. Miranda Gabriela, "2 in 5 Americans Believe Ghosts Are Real and 1 in 5 Say They've Seen One, Survey Says," *USA Today*, October 28, 2021.
73. Tony Allen-Mills, "Mothers Expect Damien on 6/6/06," *Sunday Times* (London), April 30, 2006.
74. Robert B. Stewart, Bart D. Ehrman and Daniel B. Wallace, *The Reliability of the New Testament* (Minneapolis, MN: Fortress Press, 2011), 40–41.
75. Eberhard Nestle, Erwin Nestle, Kurt Aland, et al., *Novum Testamentum Graece* (Stuttgart: Deutsche Bibelgesellschaft, 1991).

Chapter 6

76. Lynne S. McNeill and Elizabeth Tucker, *Legend Tripping: A Contemporary Legend Casebook* (Logan: Utah State University Press, 2018).
77. Goldstein, Grider and Thomas, *Haunting Experiences*, 202.
78. Ibid., 18.
79. Susa Gates, *Lydia Knight's History: The First Book of the Noble Women's Lives* (Salt Lake City, UT: Juvenile Instructor Office, 1883).
80. Ibid.
81. Ibid.
82. Ian Stevenson, "Do We Need a New Word to Supplement 'Hallucination?'" *American Journal of Psychiatry* 140, no. 12 (December 1983).

83. Grimby, "Bereavement among Elderly People," 72–80.
84. Ibid.
85. Austin E. Fife, "Popular Legends of the Mormons," *California Folklore Quarterly* 1, no. 2 (April 1942), 105–25.
86. Gerald N. Callahan, *Faith, Madness, and Spontaneous Human Combustion* (New York: Berkeley, 2003).
87. Ibid.

Chapter 7

88. Stephen L. Carr, *The Historical Guide to Utah Ghost Towns*, 3rd ed. (Salt Lake City, UT: Western Epics, 1986).
89. Quoted in Jamshid Askar, "Remembering Grafton," *Deseret News* (Salt Lake City, UT), October 24, 2009.
90. Ibid.
91. "People," National Park Service, https://www.nps.gov/zion/learn/historyculture/people.htm.
92. Ibid.
93. "Zion National Park Is Southern Paiute Land," Indigenious Geotags, March 10, 2018.
94. Western Folklife Center, "Red Rock Rondo: Back & Forth (A Ghost Story)," YouTube, October 7, 2010, https://www.youtube.com/watch?v=guDOdqaCThc.
95. Lynn McNiell, "Folklore Doesn't Meme What You Think It Memes," TEDx Talks, TEDxUSU, December 18, 2015, https://www.youtube.com/watch?v=PBDJ2UJpKt4.
96. "Vivint's Top 5 Haunted Houses in Utah," October 1, 2021, https://www.vivint.com/resources/article/vivints-top-5-haunted-houses-in-utah.
97. "Most Haunted Places in Utah," July 13, 2021, https://rvlifestyle.com/haunted-places-in-utah/.
98. "Top Five Real Haunted Places in Utah," October 2, 2020, https://skeehive.com/blogs/things-to-do-in-utah/the-top-5-real-haunted-places-in-utah.

Chapter 8

99. Huff Cates and Nancy Saphronia, "The Mountain Meadow Massacre. Statement of One of the Few Survivors," *Daily Arkansas Gazette* (Little Rock, AR), September 1, 1875. Accessed via Newspapers.com.
100. Fife, "Popular Legends of the Mormons."
101. Richard E. Turley, Janiece L. Johnson and LaJean P. Carruth, "Mountain Meadows Massacre: Collected Legal Papers," *Western Historical Quarterly* 49, no. 3 (Autumn 2018): 354–55, https://doi.org/10.1093/whq/why056.
102. W. L. Hebner, *Southern Paiute: A Portrait* (Logan: Utah State University Press, 2010).
103. Birney Hoffman, *Zealots of Zion* (Philadelphia: Penn Publishing, 1931) 196–99.
104. Morris A. Shirts, "Mountain Meadows Massacre," in *Utah History Encyclopedia*, ed. Allan Kent Powell (Salt Lake City: University of Utah Press, 1994).
105. Ronald W. Walker, "'Save the emigrants,' Joseph Clewes on the Mountain Meadows massacre (Joseph Clewes—eyewitness—Statement)," *BYU Studies* 42, no. 1 (2003): 139–52.
106. Forrest S. Cuch, *A History of Utah's American Indians* (Salt Lake City: University of Utah Press, 2003), 134.
107. Ibid., 135.
108. Juanita Brooks, *The Mountain Meadows Massacre* (Norman: University of Oklahoma Press, 1950), 214–15.
109. Casey W. Olson, "The Evolution of History: Changing Narratives of the Mountain Meadows Massacre in Utah's Public School Curricula" (PhD diss., Utah State University, 2013), https://digitalcommons.usu.edu/etd/2071.
110. "Mountain Meadows Monument," *Salt Lake (UT) Tribune*, 1874, https://newspapers.lib.utah.edu/details?id=12953398.
111. Brooks, *Mountain Meadows Massacre*, 215–16.
112. Ibid., 216.
113. Ibid., 217.
114. Goldstein, Grider and Thomas, *Haunting Experiences*, 38.
115. Brooks, *Mountain Meadows Massacre*, 214.

Chapter 9

116. Michael Bond, "The Hidden Ways That Architecture Makes You Feel," BBC, https://www.bbc.com/future/article/20170605-the-psychology-behind-your-citys-design.
117. Dickey, *Ghostland*, 18–19.

Chapter 10

118. Ibid
119. David Michael Smith, "Counting the Dead: Estimating the Loss of Life in the Indigenous Holocaust, 1492–Present," *Proceedings of the Twelfth Native American Symposium 2017*, https://www.se.edu/native-american/2017-native-american-symposium/.
120. Lifeline2170, "Possible Skin Walker Experience in Southern Utah 9-2-18. Might Have Been Followed, Please Read and Offer Any Advice/Help," https://www.reddit.com/r/skinwalkers/comments/9cehhj/possible_skin_walker_experience_in_southern_utah/.
121. Jon Tanner, "Skinwalkers," *USU Student Folklore Fieldwork*, 2017, https://digitalcommons.usu.edu/student_folklore_all/28.
122. Adrienne Keene, "Magic in North America: The Harry Potter Franchise Veers Too Close to Home," *Native Appropriations* (blog), March 7, 2016, https://nativeappropriations.com/2016/03/magic-in-north-america-the-harry-potter-franchise-veers-too-close-to-home.html.
123. K.N. Hunchman, "Stolen Spirits: The Appropriation of the Windigo Spirit in Horror Literature," *Digital Literature Review* 7 (2020), https://openjournals.bsu.edu/dlr/article/view/DLR.7.0.101-112.
124. Flannery O'Connor, "The Church and the Catholic Writer," in *Mystery and Manner* (New York: Noonday Press, 1957).
125. Hunchman, "Stolen Spirits."
126. "No Filter: Talking about Skinwalkers," *St. George News*, November 22, 2015.
127. Goldstein, Grider and Thomas, *Haunting Experiences*.

Chapter 11

128. Fife, "Popular Legends of the Mormons," 121.

129. "Augustus P. Hardy Home," Washington County Historical Society, https://wchsutah.org/homes/augustus-hardy-home.php.
130. Terry Carter, "Father Crespi and the Ancient Metallic Library," YouTube. https://www.youtube.com/watch?v=N44e6FjN5gs. (The accusation comes at the end of his presentation, minute 37:50.)
131. "Anybody's Gold Mine," *Saturday Evening Post* (Kanab, UT), October 1, 1949.
132. Richard Menzies, "Montezuma's Revenge," *Range Magazine*, 1998, https://rangemagazine.com/archives/stories/fall98/montezuma.htm.
133. Boma Johnson, Feather Robinson and Kat Johnson, "The Waterglyphs Revealed," April 2015, https://uploads.documents.cimpress.io/v1/uploads/314cd4ec-b05b-4793-a44c-ae92220db37b~110/original?tenant=vbu-digital.

ABOUT THE AUTHOR

Darren M. Edwards is a writer, photographer and educator living in Southern Utah. When he's not giving a poetry performance, busy doing a photography session, working on writing a book or teaching a class, he enjoys cuddling with his dogs, his son or his wife and, on some very magical days, all of them together.